WHAT PEOPLE ARE SAYING

You write beautifully, emotively and honestly – it's very raw. Keep writing Ms G. You are good!

Steve Matthews, Author

'Such an engaging read, I found myself intrigued by the stories shared as I found myself resonating with the feelings and struggles along Kate's life journey. The messages and teachings are strong yet subtle at the same time. I found my authentic self-awoken as I read more and more. I highly recommend this book as it truly resonated with me giving me the permission and desire to show up for myself. Thank you Kate for being brave to be vulnerable'.

Jennifer Maarseveen

'Our very own Brené Brown. How lucky are we'.

Tara Bakic

'In life, I carry a piece of Kate with me. Her energy is so infectious it brings the best out in people. She has such a special way of connecting with people and touching their core. I'm so grateful for all she's taught me over the years'.

Jo Caseley

First published by Ultimate World Publishing 2022
Copyright © 2022 Kate Glancey

ISBN

Paperback: 978-1-922828-52-1
Ebook: 978-1-922828-53-8

Kate Glancey has asserted her rights under the Copyright, Designs and Patents Act 1988 to be identified as the author of this work. The information in this book is based on the author's experiences and opinions. The publisher specifically disclaims responsibility for any adverse consequences which may result from use of the information contained herein. Permission to use information has been sought by the author. Any breaches will be rectified in further editions of the book.

All rights reserved. No part of this publication may be reproduced, stored in or introduced into a retrieval system, or transmitted in any form, or by any means (electronic, mechanical, photocopying, recording or otherwise) without the prior written permission of the author. Any person who does any unauthorised act in relation to this publication may be liable to criminal prosecution and civil claims for damages. Enquiries should be made through the publisher.

Cover design: Ultimate World Publishing
Layout and typesetting: Ultimate World Publishing
Editor: Vanessa McKay

Ultimate World Publishing
Diamond Creek,
Victoria Australia 3089
www.writeabook.com.au

DROP THE ACT

And Start Living Your Extraordinary Life!

KATE GLANCEY

DEDICATION

———————— ◆◇◆ ————————

To Mandy,

Who sees in me beyond what I see in myself.

CONTENTS

— ♦ ◇ ♦ —

Foreword	3
1. Breakthrough	7
2. Fuck!	9
3. Crossroads	15
4. Storyteller	21
5. Miss Universe	25
6. Margie	31
7. Mirror	35
8. Vision	39
9. Epiphany	43
10. Ripples	47
11. Ignorance	53
12. Bad Girl!	57
13. Coincidence...or not	61
14. Achievements	69
15. Superpowers	73
16. The Holes	81
17. The Syndrome	85
18. Expectations	91

19. I matter too!	97
20. Revolving doors	103
21. Betrayal	107
22. Connection with Spirit	113
23. Trust	119
24. Schmemmitt!	125
25. It's not about you!	129
26. Energy	135
27. Fuck again!	139
28. Loyalty	143
29. Purpose	149
30. Pure	155
31. Empowerment	159
32. Mandy	163
About the Author	169
More of what people are saying	171
References	179
Reflections	181

Life is a gift.

You can have everything you want in this life. You have the power to attract whatever you desire. You are the creator of your own experience.

We are all blessed with the opportunity to feel desire. Connecting to our deep desires leads us to our strengths. We all have strengths, each of us unique in our own way. We all have a difference, and it is our responsibility to make an impact in this world.

I believe that when you find your strengths and connect to the power of your being, you find your purpose here on this earth. You find the reason for your existence.

When I wrote this book I found a strength I had never known. The strength to show up and be seen.

I have found my purpose. To reach you, to touch you, to move you.

The pages in this book are a compilation of my stories. My experiences, my challenges and my pain. They are a reflection of my lessons and my growth. They are about me, no-one else, but me.

I have a difference and I want to make it.

FOREWORD

◆◇◆

Dear Kate,

You were always the big sister I looked up to. That we all looked up to.

Smart. Popular. Sporty.

Curly red hair for days. By the time I was old enough to realise, your hair had evolved from the long fuzzy uncool plaits that you hated, to the styled, bouncy, voluptuous curls that I so desperately envied. No amount of curl-boosting mousse scrunched into my hair helped. It didn't stop me though. Conceding that crunchy, wavy-at-best-kinks was as good as it was going to get.

You were always the big sister who drove me around. I'd sit in the front seat of your red Mitsubishi Lancer while you blasted Diesel with the windows down, singing at the top of your lungs. Admiring you as you effortlessly maneuvered the manual gearbox. Feeling the coolest I ever had, hoping that someday I'd be as good a driver as you.

You were always the big sister that braided my hair. Not inside out like Mum did - I hated that. You would spend hours meticulously

Drop The Act

weaving my hair for netball carnivals the right way, with plaits so tight they would last a week. Looking the part and feeling smug, the other girls green with envy over your masterful work.

You were always the big sister that fixed my makeup. In preparation for the oh-so-important high school party, I'd spend hours rummaging through your makeup bag trying to decipher the many foreign products that it enclosed. Lacquering everything as heavy as possible, as if it were outdoor paint. You'd catch me, then blend my eyeshadow, re-draw my eyebrows and wipe off three-quarters of what I had just applied. Feeling pretty, I walked out in awe, wondering if I'd ever know the difference between dry, wet, and powder foundation like you did.

You were always the big sister that resolved family riffs. When fights erupted in the house, you were the safe harbour I turned to. That we all turned to. You were the consigliere. Mediator. Fixer. You made everything okay.

I cried when you moved out of home. An aching pain of abandonment in my chest. Something I knew you felt too. A weight far too heavy for any sibling to carry, but one you carried for all of us.

But the sister you were to me growing up, is not the sister you are today. I don't look up to you anymore. I admire you.

I admire you for your bravery and courage for stepping out from behind the character you thought you needed to play. For your fortitude in choosing to live an authentic life. For walking down an impossibly difficult path littered with judgment and self-doubt. For turning your face into the light, unembarrassed of being seen.

Foreword

You have shed the skin of conformity that has suffocated you for years. Staring deep into the eyes of shame, bellowing out a loud resounding 'FUCK YOU!'.

You have chosen love. For yourself. In the deepest, most spiritual way.

You are the big sister I admire. Because you are you.

Love,
Amy

1

BREAKTHROUGH

––––––––––––––– ◆◇◆ –––––––––––––––

The Easter weekend of 2022 found me at Manyana, a quiet coastal town on Sydney's South Coast.

The morning light poked its way around the edge of the curtain. The ocean whispered its way through the door, gently calling me from sleep. The crisp air filled my lungs and cleared the blur from my eyes. I lay snuggled under the warmth of the blankets, pausing to notice the infusion of gratitude in my heart.

A gentle warbling sound called me to my feet. I turned back the covers and crept to the door to peer around the curtain. There he was, perched on the balcony rail, preening his wings only two feet from my door. Standing bold in his black and white magnificence. Like he had waited for my return as patiently as he now waited for his breakfast.

I stepped onto the balcony and the sting of cold tiles greeted my bare feet. I hugged the blanket tight as if to warn away the cold.

Drop The Act

The rumble of the ocean wrapped around me as I squinted slightly, restricting the glare that reflected off the white rendered walls.

I sat in the tranquillity of the morning, enjoying a rare moment of solitude. Lost in the beauty of Manyana.

'Come on, we're going to the beach', Mandy ordered. 'And you're going to write!'

'What?' I gasped as I jumped to my feet. 'Write at the beach! I can't write at the beach!'

'We're going!' she said as she gathered her book, and the multiple protective items I would be needing to sit under the Australian sun.

My brain went into overdrive. Thoughts raced through my mind. *I can't.* All those stories I had clung to so tightly that had suffocated me and had kept me from feeling my truth.

But it would be this Thursday morning, today, that I took a breath. However uncertain and unsure, I stepped back from my ego, from the beliefs I had clung to since before I had ever known any different, and paid attention to the rumble coming from deep within, roaring at me to pay attention. My soul was calling me to greater things.

'What are you going to write about?' she asked, a glimmer of pride evident in her tone, like she saw something that I didn't. 'What's the purpose of this book?'

I didn't have an answer for her. I didn't know the answer. I just knew I had to write.

2

FUCK!

---◆◇◆---

From before I knew much of anything I just knew that *fuck* was a bad word. It was a word rarely used, and rarely heard in our well-to-do semi practising Christian family.

Mum never cursed. Well, she never used *fuck* anyway. It was always obvious when Mum had reached her limit with one of us when she exclaimed 'Shit!' But it was never pronounced 'Shit!' It was more like, 'Shiiiiiiiiiiiiiiiit!' The long, overly emphasised expletive was met with the scurry of five girls, ducking for cover and running for safety from the wrath of an angry mum.

I never really understood what had made her so angry. Through the eyes of a five-year old she looked frustrated, overwhelmed, fed up. Like she had reached her limit. She had just had enough. My big person brain gets it. Now, being a mum to three boys, I get it. But back then, I didn't get it. I just felt it. The intense energy of my mum's distress vibrated through my entire being and sprung to life in the form of anxiety. My heart raced; my chest tightened

Drop The Act

but most of all I felt sick to my stomach. My frantic attempts to protect myself from the disabling feelings that came over me with a force greater than my physical body could handle, saw me develop the very effective strategy of *fixing*. I became the *fixer*! I fixed everything in an attempt to feel safe.

Dad never made a habit of using the bad words either, but on the odd occasion the Sydney traffic proved too much for his well restrained perfectly modelled demeanour. His professional practice was located in the same town where we all went to the Catholic high school, St Patrick's Ladies College. Every weekday morning, we fought one another for the use of one bathroom in order to get glammed up ready in our private school girl uniforms, hair sprayed, and make-up ever so discreetly applied, and then fight for a seat in Dad's car to avoid the harrowing bus ride to school. Catching the bus was, without a doubt the less preferred option given the awkward mix of public and private school students.

The bus ride was educational, to say the least. I learnt so many new words on the bus ride to school, words that I didn't understand, but words I was pretty sure were not conversational topics at the dinner table. 'Red-headed rat rooter', they yelled from the back seat of the bus. The kids on the back seat were always the cool kids. I never made it to the back seat of the bus. In fact, I don't think I ever made it past half-way, let alone all the way to the very back. On those dreaded mornings of forced communal travel I slid into my seat, somewhere near the front, hoping to God my bright red fuzzy hair wouldn't announce my presence, and sat with my head hung in my lap as I cringed at the thought of who I was. What was a rat-rooter anyway?

Fuck!

Dad navigated the morning peak hour traffic with great patience…most mornings. But on a good day, the frustration of the traffic, usually triggered by an incompetent driver cutting in front of Dad's red Honda Prelude saw a little hint of realness spurt out of his mouth as he cursed, 'fucken moron!'. For a reason I never thought too much about, hearing the expletive leave Dad's mouth came with a degree of humour and relief. Funny, because we never heard Dad swear. Relief, because maybe seeing the imperfection in my parent released the well tightened screw I had applied to my very own perfect pressure valve.

I held Gezza, dad, psychologist extraordinaire in such high regard. He just knew everything. On weekday evenings I sat patiently at the kitchen bench anticipating his arrival home from work when I would revel in the stories he told about the people he had met that day and the circumstances they endured. I sat in awe as I listened to story after story. I was truly fascinated.

I always knew that I wanted to be a psychologist. I wanted to be just like my dad. In my senior years at the all-girls Catholic high school I attended we were encouraged to consider our future career options. We were to find a two-week work placement within our field of interest. I remember the buzz of excitement amongst all the smart girls in class as they shared their very definite ideas of what they were going to be when they left school and where they would be completing their placement. Doctor, surgeon, paediatrician, lawyer. None of the smart girls mentioned anything about being a psychologist. *Fuck!* I thought. Psychologist must be a shit thing to be, it's definitely not the smart girl thing to be. And doing a work placement with your dad was absolutely not the cool girl thing to do. So, with feigned confidence and certainty I proudly announced that I would be pursuing law. Yes, that's right, I was going to be a lawyer!

I hadn't even made it to morning tea on my first day of placement at the local legal aid office when I plunged deep into a state of overwhelm. The same anxiety that I felt in response to my Mum's 'Shiiiiiiiiiiiit' outbursts. *What was I doing? What had I done?* I felt out of my depth and totally out of alignment with my passion, and what I later would come to realise, my purpose.

I vividly remember the day I was granted my registration to practise psychology. I felt way too little and way too young to be given a title. Like a real title. Especially one with 'ologist' at the end. Like, did they really know what they were doing, saying that I was allowed to be a real psychologist and talk to real people with real problems. In my hand, I held the fancy piece of paper that bear my name across the top, in fancy writing with a very fancy emblem. Then I joined the practice as *Gerard's daughter*.

Fuck! I thought. They are going to leave me alone with someone needing real help. *Fuck! Fake it till you make it. You only have to know more than your client and you will be right* I convinced myself. *Fuck! Fuck! Fuck!*

Although at that time I didn't know the technical term for what I was feeling, but I knew the feeling all too well. Feeling like a fraud. A fake. An imposter. The feeling that surely someone was going to find out that I'm not really a real psychologist.

Fuck became a word I used fondly and regularly. A word that seemed to accurately reflect my internal turmoil. It was like the word *fuck* was designed especially for me, for the countless moments I

Fuck!

found myself buried deep in self-doubt. For the many moments I had followed my ego driven expectation of who I thought I should be, rather than who I truly was.

3

CROSSROADS

───────── ◆◇◆ ─────────

For me marriage is a bit like sport. When you choose a life partner you join the same team. You register for the same club, and you wear the same strip. You form loyalties and bonds within the team and those loyalties extend to the club in which you belong. You wear the colours with pride. You breathe the colours of your tribe.

Sometimes within our team we fight. We disagree. We butt heads. We work against our common goals. We lose our way. But if we continue to show up in the colours that represent our club, we always find our way home.

When you separate, you quit the team. Or maybe you quit the team, then you separate. But either way, you can't just be on no team. It is without intention, (or at least it wasn't my intention) that you find yourselves on opposing teams.

Hindsight is a wonderful thing that sharpens our vision like nothing you can buy in a Spec Savers store. When I separated, people asked me questions like 'Why?', 'What happened?' In the eyes of my questioning friends, I could see their anticipation as they waited for me to provide a dramatic story justifying my decision to leave. I found myself lost for an answer. Without the convenience of any one dramatic event to shove the blame one way or another, I had to wonder myself. *What really did go wrong?* I looked back over many moments in my marriage trying to piece together some form of coherent story that would make sense to those that cared to ask.

I've played sport for as long as I can remember. Netball was my first choice of sport. Well to be honest, I think netball was my mum's first and only choice of sport for the five of us. I remember dreaming of becoming a dancer when I was little. Every Sunday morning, I woke early and raced downstairs to the lounge room, tuning in to channel 2 to catch the music hits program Rage. I danced and I sang, totally in tune of course, and dreamed of being just like one of them. Sometimes my sisters would join me, and we would choreograph our own dance, each of us engrossed in our own delusional image of being a real famous dancer. Needless to say, my dancing career never took off. Mum never took me to dance school. My dreams of becoming a dancer were never to become a reality.

So, netball it was. Mum played netball, my sisters played netball, we all played netball. Every Saturday morning I got up early, dressed in my bottle green skirt and white scrunched socks, feeling like I had transformed into someone else. Pretending I was someone else. Dreaming of being someone else.

Netball and dancing weren't so dissimilar after all. It was the ability to lose myself in my own idealised perception that I loved. As a dancer I was gracious and free. In my perfectly pleated netball skirt, I was also gracious and free. It is the purity and innocence of our childlike self that is so adoring. And with life's challenges I found myself losing connection with my innocence more and more as time moved forward.

Everything that is meant for us will come to us. Dancing never came to me. Obviously, dancing was never meant for me and my path in this life. I can still hear my Mum's comments on the side line of the netball court.

'You sound like an elephant running up and down that court'.

Although I didn't believe it then, but now, when I look at the size of my well-built thighs, I do believe the universe closed the dancing door on me for a greater reason.

The idea that I was gifted with solid thighs for a reason greater than dancing was lost on me for many years. What kind of gift is that to give a female? Dad used to say:

'You got those from me. Sorry pet!', followed by a hearty chuckle.

Sorry pet, my ass! I thought.

We were a sporty family. Mum and Dad both played sports well into their adult years. It was quite the thrill to be out and about on a school night at Bankstown Basketball stadium. Mum dragged us along every week, five kids in tow, rugged up in dressing gowns and Ugg boots. The energy of the stadium was electric. The sounds of balls bouncing, teammates chatting and whistles blowing was chaotic and exhilarating. The energy

Drop The Act

of being part of something, part of a game, part of a team was super cool. However, at some stage I came to realise that turning up in my dressing gown and Ugg boots was absolutely not cool.

'When are you going to come and give footy a go?', Dad asked in his subtle yet not so subtle way of pushing me into something new.

He had this way of dropping a challenge right in my lap, leaving me with this newfound awareness of how happy I was to avoid vulnerability at all costs and keep myself small. Seriously, just let me stay ignorantly unaware of all the scary things that might not be so scary if I just gave it a go. My BFF imposter syndrome totally had my back. She barracked for me with great conviction. *Don't you listen to him! What would he know anyway. You can't play football. You will be humiliated if you even try that dumb sport. And besides, the ball is a dumb shape and doesn't even bounce properly.*

It took a few weeks, ok maybe a few years before I reluctantly agreed to give footy a go. My BFF had taken a temporary absence of leave and in a moment of weakness, I signed up.

Fuck! Fuck! Fuck!

I loved footy. Well obviously, I didn't love footy the first time I played. I panicked and sent an SOS to my BFF who of course, rushed back from her leave of absence to be with me at my first ever game. She was committed!

I would go on to play footy for the next 27 years. I still play footy now. I do love footy. I had found the reason I was gifted solid thighs. Somewhere along the line, after numerous selections for representative teams and national level representation, my BFF and I broke up. It was a long drawn-out breakup, it took a lot of convincing. But it was time.

When I found myself no longer on the same team as my husband, I felt more lost and alone than ever. There was no blame to be had, there was no dramatic story. We had stopped showing up in our team colours. I was scared, no I was absolutely petrified of what it meant to not be on the same team anymore. I didn't want to not be on the same team anymore.

Separation is hard. Separating finances is really hard. Drawing the comparison between the loss of a partner through separation versus the loss of a partner through death is a discussion I've had with several clients over the years. And in every one of these conversations the separated person has considered that, the loss of a partner through death would have been easier to endure than the loss of a partner who continues living. I cannot attest to the pain of losing a partner through death, but I can attest to the pain of losing a partner through life.

I sat in the office of a family lawyer who I had employed to finalise the paperwork side of our financial separation.

'Are you sure you don't want to keep the commercial property, it would be a great investment!,' he interrogated across the antique rosewood table.

This was not the first conversation I'd had regarding the sale of this property.

Drop The Act

'I urge you to consider keeping the office, wealthy people don't sell properties, they keep them!', Dad had said as he attempted to persuade me to do what he thought was best for me.

I had spent my entire life navigating my way through meeting the expectations of what other people thought I should do, what they thought was best for me. I had always listened. In the office of my family law solicitor, I listened.

As I stepped out of his office and into the jacaranda-lined street of the country town where I had spent my childhood, I stopped suddenly like someone, or something had put brakes on my feet. I stopped and I listened. I'm not sure if it was the universe talking to me, or my gut telling me, or maybe they are one and the same. But I listened. And I heard. And I saw with great clarity what I needed to do for me.

4

STORYTELLER

––––––––––––––◆◇◆––––––––––––––

I met Mandy in my early years of playing football. She was good at footy, really good. And I wasn't. She wasn't someone who, on first meeting seemed friend material for me. She was well established in the football scene. In my eyes she was strong, confident, and self-assured, maybe a little or even a lot arrogant, all the qualities that seemed scary and intimidating to me. I didn't like her too much. I didn't like how I felt when I was around her. Being in her energy seemed to shine a spotlight right into the parts of me that I desperately wanted to hide, feeling weak, underconfident and totally unsure. But I had become an expert, a master at my well perfected trade of hiding within myself, hiding the parts of me I didn't like much and faking it. Even though on the inside I felt small and exposed, I stepped into the confident character of fun loving, self-assured, totally unbothered, and easy-going Kate, and I did it so easily. It was like a knee jerk reaction for me.

Tuesday nights saw us gather together at Minto Touch football association for our weekly game of touch footy. I started my touch

Drop The Act

football career with a team of young ladies who were gracious enough to take me under their wing, despite my tendency to want to merge my well drilled netball skills into the game of touch football. Getting touched whilst carrying the ball in my hands and passing the ball forwards were not only basic, but highly encouraged skills on a netball court. The sound of the referee's whistle blown into my ear each time the ball came my way, left me wondering what I had done wrong.

'You can't throw the ball once you've crossed over the try line. And you can't throw it forward.' One of the girls explained making little attempt to hide her frustration at my ignorance for the rules of my newfound sport.

'Oh okay,' I said, making every effort to hide the embarrassment I felt creep up into my face and turn my pale skin a shade of pink, feeling hopeful that my truth would be hidden in the darkness of the night. *Stupid fucken game! Who made up the rule that you have to pass the ball backwards anyway? Stupid game!*

For a reason that I could draw absolutely no sense from at that time, I was asked to play in a second team. By other people. Other real football people. *Fuck* I thought. *Do they actually know who I am, and that I can't play this dumb game? Half the time I don't even know what direction I'm supposed to be running.*

Playing two games on one night, in a competition running three time slots meant that we often found ourselves with a break between games. Some reason somehow, I found myself gathering amongst a group of girls who were really good at football. Like good enough to be asked to play in two teams because they actually know how to pass the odd shape ball backwards. They were way too good at football to be my friends. But they were gracious enough to allow me to hang out with them for the 45-minute break before the next demonstration of athletic skill would be displayed for all to see.

'Tell us the story about that person you met the other week,' Mandy pleaded. Despite my bewilderment as to why they wanted to hear something I had to say, I cooperated. 'You always tell the best stories,' she said.

I had always jumped at any chance to hear my dad tell stories of people. My dad had a way of weaving humour into the most serious and heavy of stories involving people and the misfortunes of human life. I had inherited his skill of storytelling. I was a storyteller. And so every Tuesday night, in the freezing cold temperatures of winter and the muggy nights of the Australian summer, I sat with an audience of the really good football girls entertaining them. Still to this day, Mandy talks about those nights when I told the best stories. I told those stories with delight. Delight that the girls loved my stories, and delight at the thought that maybe they loved me.

Mandy was a complicated individual. She was strong and confident, at least on the outside anyway. Although often triggered by her less than inviting ways, I found myself drawn to her. Much like the workings of a magnet, there was a competing energy of attraction and repulsion arising between the charge of motion between us. It was a long time coming before I would understand the magnetic force that existed in the space between her and I. And a long time coming before I liked her a little bit more than I did in those early football days.

5

MISS UNIVERSE

──────── ◆◇◆ ────────

The Catholic Club was the best worst job I could have landed at the age of 18. I studied during the week and when the weekend rolled around, I worked. My friends flocked to the bar and threw their weekly savings at Jim Beam and Jack Daniels. They played and I worked.

Working long hours on weekends meant lots of time away from home. Leaving a depressed mother at home alone, dressed in pyjamas at times of the day that spoke clearly of her energy for life, tore strips at my heart, a pain that haunted me deeply. Work served as a healthy distraction. But at the end of every shift, often at ungodly hours of the morning, I returned home, driving down the winding driveway of Berry Close where our once complete family of seven had built the dream home.

When Dad left, he left us with everything. The eight and a half acres, the dogs, the horses, and the motor bikes. I knew even back then that walking away empty handed was his best effort at easing

Drop The Act

the guilt he carried for choosing himself. A guilt I knew ran deep through his veins and buried its way into the marrow of his bones.

Jess came into this world as the baby of the Glancey girls. Family of five. Complete! Emma and I were the proud adoring big sisters. We played with Jess like she was our very own Baby Born doll, pushing her around in a stroller and wrapping her up in her very own blankie. I can only imagine what happened in Jess's three-year-old brain when, on dad's 36th birthday in 1983, only two weeks after Jess turned three, Mum disappeared to the hospital and four days later two more babies arrived home.

The twins, Amy and Beth came home without Mum. Dad's niece Lisa came to stay with us, to look after us, and for all I knew, this was a fun sleep over with our big cousin. We were too little to know, but Mum remained in hospital under observation for what doctors considered might be a brain tumour. She was suffering debilitating headaches, migraines, and would undergo rigorous testing to seek the answers for these bewildering symptoms. Nothing was found. Nothing that the medical professionals were willing to diagnose. So, she just came home. Well, her physical body came home. There was a part of her that never came home.

When Dad left, something moved in with us. It was a heavy black cloud that enveloped every cell in mum's body and every inch of her soul. She left again. Or maybe she had never really come back. I don't know. But I did know that every time I left the house after Dad had gone, I felt it. Whatever it was that Dad had taken, I felt it. It was like I became a lifeline, an energy source that gave her just enough to meet only the basic human needs of survival. We were in survival mode.

Miss Universe

I was more than aware of my responsibility for my Mum's ability to continue taking breaths in her less than willing quest to survive. Maybe it was my only way to survive but what I didn't see, or maybe couldn't bear to see, was the heaviness that my baby sisters carried when I abandoned my responsibility to my mum, taking that energy source with me every time I left the house. The weight they carried was immense and would leave traces on their soul.

The universe has her own way of guiding us along the path towards our greatest good. It has only been in the most recent years that I have discovered the awe of this higher power. She has been here all along, I truly believe that. She has offered me the most valuable lessons and made all efforts to guide me to where I'm meant to be. But I haven't made it easy on her, so I guess I shouldn't be pissed when she doesn't take it easy on me. That's the thing with us humans, it takes really big things for us to hear.

Back at the beach on day two of the Easter long weekend, we were accompanied by Gezza and his blonde haired, blue-eyed love of his life, Rosie the labradoodle. Because five daughters hadn't provided enough feminine hysteria in his life so far. Also in tow were the Beanos, the tightly run ship of four led by the baby of the family, Betty.

Betty has the most beautiful loving warm and inviting energy of anyone you would ever meet. Often referred to as 'the nice twin', Betty is a beam of brightness, sprinkling shards of light everywhere she goes. She is like a natural energy source of love and light equipped with endless supplies of brightness that burst from her soul.

Drop The Act

This Easter weekend at Manyana it was like Betty didn't show up, she wasn't here. The brightness, the sparkle, the sprinkling shards of light were gone. She still smiled on the outside and said all the Betty things. She still acted like Betty, but she didn't feel like Betty. She was gone.

She played the part well. She kept her commitment to the Betty character, the Betty she must have felt we all wanted her to be, or that she felt she needed to be. But I could see beyond the surface, I could see through her. I could feel her at a deeper level. And I felt her pain.

Betty has two amazing little boys, Hugo and Leo. Hugo, a strong determined being forging his own unique path in life. Leo, cautious and sensitive, a deep feeler. In amongst the delightful chaos of the supposed relaxing break, Betty took one of the few kid free moments to grab my attention.

'I want to tell you something and I don't want you to judge me,' she started. Her pain flashed through me like a lightning bolt as I sat with her on the beach, Hugo and Leo digging in the sand. Nothing else mattered to me in this moment, my heart was connected to her heart, and I could feel the deadness that had taken residence in her heart space. My heart ached for her, it was like a squeezing suffocating energy tightened in my chest causing a heavy ache.

Betty is a successful life doer. On the outside, she had it all. She was the kind of attractive that pleased the eyes of her many Instagram followers. Being an identical twin, who almost always featured by her side on her Instagram page, only added to the attention of curious admirers. She had achieved the kind of success that provided huge bragging rights for any admiring sister. Managing director of a cute funky makeup company, general manager of the country's biggest makeup distributor, whilst rejecting offers from one of the world's most admired jewellery companies. Betty had it all. Well, so it seemed.

Life had come to a head for Betty. The universe long since quit whispering to her, she was now screaming, she meant business. Betty was broken and it was time. As I sat with her on the beach under the warm autumn sun, I held the space she needed to share a realness I had never before heard come out of her mouth. She was raw and she was real. She shared her pain. She shared her truth. She stepped into her greatest vulnerability and asked for help.

We are all looking for love. We are biologically wired this way. We spend our lives looking, searching, grasping from people, partners, and things. What we are truly looking for lies deep within all of us, love comes from within. We can never truly feel for another what we can't feel within ourselves.

6

MARGIE

––––––––––––––– ◆◇◆ –––––––––––––––

When I heard social researcher Brené Brown talk about 'The Midlife Unravelling' I was stopped dead in my tracks. She says, 'Midlife is when the universe gently places her hands upon your shoulders, pulls you close, and whispers in your ear, I'm not screwing around. All of this pretending and performing…has to go. You were born worthy of love and belonging. Courage and daring are coursing through your veins. You were made to live and love with your whole heart. It's time to show up and be seen'.[1] *Yes! 100% Yes!* Brené had used the perfect words to describe the big energetic shift that I had been living. It was a thing I didn't know was happening at the time, but now looking back I see it as clear as day.

I do believe we are put on this earth for great purpose, and from the day we take our first breath we are guided by a higher power. But we are born into a human body with a highly complex brain and an impeccable capacity to think. From well before we can remember, our conscious mind seeks to define a sense of self, our identity. Our ego, our definition of who we think we are.

Drop The Act

So, who are we before our ego is born? Are we just nothing and no one until we create a story about who we think we are?

We are born in the heart space of love. There is no story and no ego. There is just love. But we are born to other humans, other humans who have long since lost connection with their space of pure love and have come to rely heavily on their own ego, their own story of who they are in order to navigate their emotional journey through life.

Worthiness is a birth right, not something you earn, not something you work for.[2] Worthiness is the gift of life.

We are biologically wired for love and connection. This part is science. We are made this way. But we are also wired to develop the ego. In our childhood developmental years, as early as two or three, we begin the journey of finding ourselves through our ego. The humans who have birthed us or have cared for us in these highly influential times set the stage for this learning platform. The ego begins its best work through experiences of fear and loss of love and connection. It is the story we create from the emotions we experience when we just don't know any better. When we are ill equipped to detach from the influence of other human beings' egos. When we are only ever doing our best, the ego stories begin, and so too does the separation from our heart space, in a desperate bid to define 'Who am I?'

In the world of psychology, we talk about attachment styles. Attachment theory is based around the concept of how we develop our relationships with other humans. It is the relationship, or attachment to our most significant caregivers that influence our social and emotional development. In a relationship where our emotional needs are not met, the avoidant attachment style is born. We shut off our own emotional needs in an attempt to stay connected to the emotionally absent human.

Dad's expressions of love were probably not atypical for a man back in the day. In fact, he was probably more loving than other dads whose egos fell much further into the category of the typical male. Dad would often place his arm across the back of my shoulders, squeeze them tight and declare, 'Love ya maaaate'. Mate was a term Dad often deferred to when he couldn't remember someone's name. It was most often used when he unexpectedly crossed the path of an acquaintance or a client in a non-related setting, like his favourite Chinese restaurant where we ate when we did go out as a family.

Mum never said, 'I love you', well not until many years later anyway.

Nanny Keech, mum's mum, lay critically ill in the hospital bed that would see her through her final days. Margie was quite the inscrutable character. She was hard to read. I have no doubt she had a heart, but she certainly did not wear it on her sleeve. Amy, Betty, and I visited her in the hospital, unaware of how unwell she was. None of us were aware.

They say that people have this sense of knowing that their final moment is nearing. I stood at the end of her bed, engaging in the smallish talk that fills the space between people when emotional realness is unfamiliar, untrodden territory. On some level I must have known. I found myself unable to move my feet towards the door as we wound up our visit. There was a pull from within, a pull I can't explain, but out of my mouth I blurted:

Drop The Act

'I love you, Nanny.'

'Righto,' she replied, bursting the emotional energy exchange I had offered, like a pin prick to a balloon. She never said 'I love you' either.

Long ago I learned to shut off my own emotional needs. Through my own experiences of fear and loss of love and connection I started creating stories. Stories of who I had to be to feel the love and connection I needed. I didn't realise I was pretending and performing. I didn't realise that I didn't feel from the pure space of my heart. You don't know what you don't know.

It takes courage to admit you are on the wrong path. To realise you are consumed with things that do not serve you well. I needed to admit I was wrong and to accept that something had to change. The universe was whispering, and I was starting to hear. No more screwing around. It is time to find the courage to drop the act, show up and be real.

7

MIRROR

At the age of 22, Amy and Betty moved to the big smoke in pursuit of a more adventurous life. Sydney was more than 70 kilometres from our quiet hometown of Camden. As kids we never ventured far from home. Dad's favourite Chinese restaurant and the annual Camden show was all the excitement we needed to feel like we were living a big life. But Amy and Betty were chasing more.

When the girls moved beyond the 10km radius from home, for all I knew they could have been in another country. It felt like they were so far away.

As they set out on their journey under the safety of each other's wings, I was at home setting up life within the acceptable radius. The six years between our birth dates had never felt more apparent. I started my family. They started their careers.

If there is one thing in life that will bond you to another, regardless of difference in age, it's kids. When Betty birthed her first child Hugo,

Drop The Act

my first child had already turned ten. A new nephew provided the perfect excuse to venture outside the radius zone and into the world beyond my little country town. When Betty birthed her second son Leo, one off visits were replaced by weekend getaways, often in Manyana.

I have always felt, that of all my sisters, Betty and I were the most similar. The answer to my somewhat inappropriate question by each unsuspecting boyfriend had always been the same. 'If you weren't with me, which sister would you choose to date?'. They tried not to be weirded out.

I saw so much of myself in Betty, and so much of Betty in myself. In any attempt to better understand myself, or see myself from someone's else's shoes, I would just step into Betty's. In many ways, Betty and I were like a mirror to one another. We were both over givers in our mission to please. We had both perfected the nice girl character in our pursuit of love. We were both loving from our ego.

Weekends away saw me spending more hours with Betty and her kids than just the few involved in a day trip to her home in the eastern suburbs.

Hugo is a tornado in human form, with steadfast determination and the smarts to get what he wants. Leo has the heart of a lion, wears it on his sleeve and lives in a vessel big enough to house it.

Hugo and Leo had both picked Betty to be their mum in this life for great reason. A reason to which, she was oblivious. Hugo demanded through stubborn negotiations and the cleverest of defiance tactics to have things work his way. Leo demanded through outbursts of emotions, sometimes heartfelt and sometimes calculated. They both demanded from their mum. In their own way, they were both trying to teach her something.

'Attention seeking,' slipped out of Dad's mouth in his attempt to shed light on the behaviour we had all witnessed many times over. Dad was right. Hugo and Leo were both seeking something from their mum. They were seeking pure love and deep connection, something their mum, who had perfected the art of loving through her ego, was not able to give.

Our greatest teachers in life often come in the form of a child. Children are born in the heart space of pure love. They know nothing more. They seek to maintain the equilibrium of love and connection. When love is removed or connection is lost, they play the part to trigger our pain. The pain blocking us from our own heart space, our own love and connection.

8

VISION

——————— ◆◇◆ ———————

In recent years I found the practice of meditation. The meditative state allows the mind to transcend the process of thought and tap into intuition. Intuition is the process of accessing information without conscious thought. It is that feeling deep in your gut when you just know.

I do believe we are all guided by a force greater than we see or know. We can't see the force, we can't always explain or reason our way through the force, we just feel it. It is some sort of knowing that shows up in the deepest part of who we are to keep us moving on our path. Feeling from my gut had long ago been smothered by my ego. My thinking brain, my storytelling chitter chatter is who or what I listened to. Constantly navigating myself and the humans around me to meet the needs and expectations of my ego.

When you want to grow beyond the ego and into your heart space, when you want to find your truth, the universe will send you everything you need to heal. She will send you the pain of

Drop The Act

abandonment to heal your lack of self-love, she will send you failure to heal your desperate need for control. She will send you the pain of lies and deception to heal the deceit you hold within yourself.

Humans who bring pain and suffering into our lives are our greatest teachers. These humans are just playing their part to gift us the opportunity to heal. When we ignore these gifts and reject the opportunity to learn, to heal, and to grow, the universe will gift us again...and again and again. After all, she does have our greatest good at play.

The journey of finding my truth, my connection to what some people call God, the universe, or our higher consciousness, I believe, will continue until the day I die. We never stop growing.

But to grow we need the challenges. We need discomfort, we need pain. We need to be pushed into our deepest wounds to find what we need within, to find what we need to heal.

Mandy used to see me as someone who didn't worry about anything. I didn't get upset and I didn't cry. She said I had it all together. For the most part I sat in a blissful ignorance, consciously believing that I did in fact, mostly, not totally, but mostly, have it all together. I was a psychologist, and my job was to help navigate people towards the space where they could reason their way through their emotions and ultimately achieve the goal of an even keel. The intense emotional reactions that were far from my usual even keel, to me, seemed dramatic and immature.

But I had asked. I had asked the universe to feel. I wanted to feel.

Vision

Feeling something when you don't feel it seemed bizarre to me. I questioned, *How can you feel it if you can't feel it?* This is where the universe steps in and gently, or more often brutally, sends you what you need.

It was a full moon. Mandy and I sat under the brightly lit ball of light suspended in amongst the dazzling stars of the night sky. We chatted, well I chatted, and she listened. We gazed at the moon and were wowed by the beauty of our universe. When Mandy got sick of my chatting, without grace, tact, or any beating around the bush, she shooshed me. It was time to Rapé.

Mandy often got feelings. She was connected and grounded and highly attuned to her gut and the messages she was being shown.

'I feel like something big is coming,' she said.

These words were always met with a mix of fear and excitement, for I knew she was always right. We set the intention to surrender and accept the lesson, the greater good of what this big thing would bring. *Don't fight it, surrender.*

Rapé is a sacred shamanic spiritual practice that has been used for hundreds of years by tribes in the Amazon to release energy from the body, ground and connect. The men of tribes often used Rapé before a hunting adventure to open the intuition and enhance clarity. That night we sat in ceremony under the intense energy of the full moon with the intention of surrender and clarity.

What Mandy saw and felt that night, through every inch of her body, brought her to her knees. She felt overwhelmingly nauseous. She wanted to vomit. Her stomach convulsed as she

Drop The Act

dry wretched, but she did not purge. She did not release. This was not an emotional pain she was carrying that could be released in ceremony. This was a vision of something to come.

'I feel like this is for you,' she said. 'I feel like it is around your mum.'

When we want to work harder and go deeper, we need real life things to bring us pain. I had set the intention to feel, and to feel deeply. What could possibly need to happen to plunge me into a state of deep despair, to cause me pain that would bring me to my knees.

Fuck, I thought.

9

EPIPHANY

◆◇◆

The trip home from Manyana was made even shorter by the conversation that followed on from our time with the family over the Easter weekend.

'This book is going to do great things,' Mandy said. 'I can feel the ripple effect has already started'.

On the morning of our departure, Mandy set up the Bowen table on the northeast facing verandah, overlooking the stretch of ocean that sat quietly beneath the sherbet sky that greeted me each morning. The mention of the word Bowen coming from Mandy's mouth saw a burst of energy and enthusiasm spring to life in Betty's legs, causing an almost involuntary leap from where she sat on the lounge, swiftly moving her body across the room towards where the Bowen table awaited her arrival. She assumed the position with as much surrender as a Buddhist monk in a temple of worship, awaiting the touch of Mandy's strong but gentle healing hands. Another thing Betty and I had in common.

Drop The Act

She lay face down succumbing to the release of emotional pain she had clung to without choice or awareness for the years of her life that extended beyond her conscious memory. I read to her the pages I had written in the days before. My voice quivered. The tears that welled in my eyes spilled down my cheeks. I took more deliberate breaths than would ordinarily be required to get through a few lines of a book. As she lay face down on the bed, her body lifeless and without movement, she sniffled. She sniffled again, and then she sobbed.

In the early 1900s the psychological breakdown was viewed as the commonly experienced overwhelm of the everyday individual resulting from the challenges of the everyday life. You weren't mad, the world was! I don't know when this changed but our modern-day world holds little space for the commonplace overwhelm of the everyday woman or man. We have come to fear the madness that comes from a world that we have created. Without the madness of the life we have been gifted, there is no breakdown. And without permission to breakdown, there is no breakthrough.

As Betty lay sobbing, feeling and releasing, she was breaking. Breaking down. Breaking down the barriers and the layers and the blocks that had robbed her of feeling. Robbed her of feeling pain, sadness and despair. Robbed her of feeling love. Robbed her of feeling connection. She was breaking through.

'I think I've had an epiphany,' Betty shared. 'I can see that it's me. I suppress what I feel so much that I don't even know it's there. I live in my ego and not in my heart.'

For the first time Betty stopped looking outwards and she looked in. She looked at her ego, the stories she had created to feel safe.

Epiphany

The stories that helped her avoid pain. She found the courage to visit her pain and she owned her own shit.

'I can't wait to fall in love with Deano all over again,' she said.

'But first Betty, you must fall in love with yourself.'

When we try and control our world, control everyone and everything around us, we create for ourselves a delusional existence. We create stories and stories create beliefs. We defend our beliefs to feel safe. When we remain caged in our beliefs we suffer. But when we do the work on ourselves, everything around us starts to shift. Everything starts to change.

10

RIPPLES

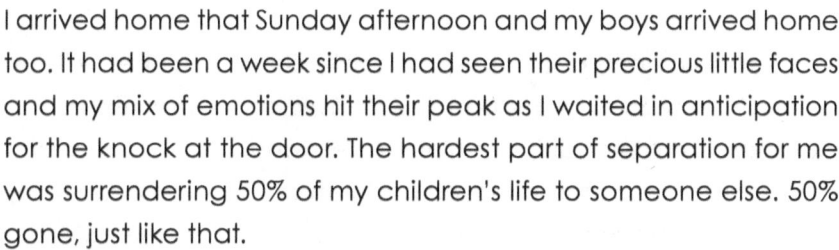

I arrived home that Sunday afternoon and my boys arrived home too. It had been a week since I had seen their precious little faces and my mix of emotions hit their peak as I waited in anticipation for the knock at the door. The hardest part of separation for me was surrendering 50% of my children's life to someone else. 50% gone, just like that.

Their arrival home saw an outpouring of emotion, from me to them, and from them to me. It's like a release of grief and sadness and loss, mixed in with joy and happiness and more joy, all bundled up in one. Those cuddles are the absolute best, and it is times like these I wish my gift at birth would have been six arms rather than the thighs already mentioned, so I could hold each one of them, at exactly the same time, for as long as they needed.

'I missed you,' Harry said. He didn't need to say much, but in that brief moment, a moment I wish I had captured on my boom box

Drop The Act

tape recorder so I could rewind and replay it a thousand times over, I felt those few words had come from his heart.

Evidence of the Easter Bunny's presence was spewed throughout the lounge room, the kitchen, and the boys' bedrooms. Jack and Charlie gasped as they collected the bright coloured eggs in the breakfast bowls they had pinched from the kitchen drawer. Their delight was most evident as they expressed their disbelief that not only did the Easter Bunny know they loved Sonic and Marvel, but he had been generous enough to leave them a new winter onesie together with matching undies.

'Thanks Mum,' Harry said with a grin indicative of his willingness to keep the secret.

Macie and Emmitt came to share Easter Sunday dinner with us, as did Nanny Sue, aka Mum. The conversation was rife as the kids shared the shenanigans of their weekends away, Macie and Emmitt's stories a little more colourful than those shared by my kids. None of my kids' stories included 'Goon of Fortune' drinking games, headaches and hangovers, nor having played a part in the arrest of a local drug dealer in the country pub where apparently, clothing was not considered necessary for entry.

Nanny Sue loves to tell a story. She loves it so much she will tell you the same one over and over. I guess it comes with having five daughters. She can never remember who has already heard the story. So, at any risk of it not having been you, she will tell it to you again...and sometimes again, just in case.

'Rissoles,' I blurted, abruptly interrupting a story I had already had the pleasure of hearing, more than once. 'Rissoles' was the code word we used to bring awareness to Mum's habit of repeating and retelling.

'Oh, shut up you!', she said as she continued the story.

'You've already told me this one,' I said.

'Oh, have I?' she laughed, as she continued with the more than familiar details of the story.

Mum asked about our weekend away. She asked about the girls and the grandkids. About whether Linda, Dad's partner was at Manyana. Secretly, I still think there's a niggling wound between Mum and Linda. Or possibly it is just Mum's incessant need to know every detail of everything about everyone.

It was a moment I recognised in the moment. It took me straight back to Mandy's vision and I felt sick to the stomach. Mum asked me about Betty. *Fuck!*

My immediate reaction was to cover and downplay the truth I had learned that weekend. In this family, we share a lot. In fact, we overshare. We share poo stories and bowel movements. We share prolapses and pants peeing. But we don't share truth. When it comes to the real shit, we get a rug and a broom, and we sweep like there's no tomorrow. This is a family habit we do really well. But in my pursuit of being real, I couldn't pretend. And I couldn't lie. I had to speak the truth. So, I told her the truth about Betty. I told her Betty was broken. Even though I knew this would cause her pain, I told her. Even though I knew this would cause me pain, I told her.

Drop The Act

I also told her I was writing a book. In anticipation of her doubt and scepticism, I followed with, 'Actually, I have already started writing a book.'

She kind of laughed, seemed kind of confused. 'What about?' she asked.

'Me, my stuff, life...you know!'

Mandy, Macie, and Emmitt left to return home to Elm Lodge, their magnificent property located in the even smaller-than-Camden town of Oakdale. Oakdale have just refurbished and reopened their local football club, a monumental moment for the most patriotic locals you would expect to meet in a town of such size.

Nanny Sue stayed for a little while longer. Well, for anyone who knows Nanny Sue, it was actually a lot longer.

'Read me what you wrote about Betty.'

FUCK! This shit is getting real!!!!!

We sat at my kitchen table, just Mum and I, and I read to her the words describing the internal pain of her daughter's anguish. Reading the words out loud, the words I had written of my Mum's pain and Betty's pain, conjured strong emotion within me. My breaths became deliberate, my words controlled as I struggled to share the enormity of the emotion behind the sentences on the page. I finished the chapter. I took a breath, a breath that struggled under the weight of my chest. I looked up from the page, my vision blurred by the tears that welled, yet unwilling to fall until my eyes met hers, and the tears spilled over.

Ripples

It has taken a lot of work, me doing the work on me, to get me here. To get me to where I am right now. To have found the things that I need within me. To show up for myself. To write my truth. To share my truth.

And here I am. Right where I am meant to be. Watching the ripples as they play out in front of me.

11

IGNORANCE

◆ ◇ ◆

Writing a book was never something I thought I could or would do. When I was a young psychologist, about 22 years of age, I booked an appointment with a well-known psychic. She had a long-standing reputation in our local area, known for her craft of seeing the present and predicting the future. As is common practice for all of us sceptics, I booked the appointment under my first name only, as I knew that giving away my surname would make it easy to identify my profession, particularly as we both worked in the same town.

From the moment I arrived I felt drawn to her space. Rose bushes left untrimmed spewed over an ageing white picket fence. A stone cobbled path led to the statement-coloured front door. An array of plants sprinkled randomly around the haven that was her home. The mix of pattern and texture in the soft furnishings a reflection of her spirit, unconventional and free. A scattering of trinkets hinted at the adventures of her time.

Drop The Act

'You're very psychological,' she stated before I'd even had time to take a seat.

I don't remember much about what she told me that day, but I do remember that much of what she told me made me feel that either a) she had managed to somehow work out who I was, where I lived, what I did for a profession and what colour undies I chose to wear every day, or b) she had an amazing gift that surpassed my brain's logical ability to comprehend.

'I can see you writing,' she said.

Confident in my naive belief that I knew exactly what she was talking about, 'Oh yes,' I replied. 'I write a lot of reports in my work.'

'No, that's not what I'm seeing. You're going to write a book,' she said confidently.

I was so taken by the amount of information she had already accurately relayed about me and my life, that I found myself willing to forgive her for the apparent error in judgment.

'I guess she can't get everything right.'

Years later I was sitting in front of another psychic. I recall even less from the hour that I spent listening to her recount details of my past, present and future.

'You're going to have twins,' she said. 'But there will be a gap between your first child and these babies'.

Ignorance

Two years of failed IVF attempts after an easy conception with my first child had left me desperately clinging to the hope she offered in that reading when she told me that two more babies would come to me.

'And I see you writing a book,' she added. That information barely caught my attention. I only cared about the promised babies I so desperately wanted.

12

BAD GIRL!

––––––––––––––– ◆◇◆ –––––––––––––––

In 2021 I received an email from the Health Care Complaints Commission, the regulatory body for all health professionals in New South Wales. I don't recall the words themselves, but I do recall the scolding energy of the bold black capital letters on the subject line of the email, demanding my attention in a reprimanding manner like a naughty Catholic school girl being castigated for speaking in church.

'Oh my god,' I blasphemed to myself, 'What have I done wrong?'

A complaint had been raised against me for professional misconduct by a man whom I had never met, never seen nor ever spoken with. Like seriously, if you are going to have a professional complaint raised against you, this would surely be the best one to have right! *Right?* I tried to convince myself. My logical brain did its utmost best to relieve me of my concerns, but my anxiety brain had taken centre stage, microphone in hand like an intoxicated stay-at-home mother of five let loose

Drop The Act

on her first girls' night out in a sleazy underground karaoke bar in King's Cross.

'What have I done wrong? she pestered, 'I must have done something wrong?'

The well accepted belief in my 'wrong-doing actions' were the cause of great anxiety and allowed the vicious cycle of self-doubt to flourish like a moss in deep shade. Self-doubt is the greatest self-limiting belief that you can attach yourself to.

I had clung to this self-limiting belief for all the years of my life, like the tenacious suction of a clingfish to rock. Fun fact: I never knew what a clingfish was until I started writing this book, but I have since learned that the clingfish's powerful suction ability enables them to cling to rocks despite the power of battering waves. Their unique ability provided inspiration in the development of an artificial suction cup, the prototype even more superior. I was the prototype.

I lived my life in great pursuit of always doing the right thing. I thought that doing the right thing was the right thing to do. I thought it made me a good person. A person worthy of love. So, when I didn't do the right thing, on rare occasions, I met a new friend. Shame.

Shame didn't really like it when I was doing the right thing and being an all-round goodie-two-shoes, so we didn't actually spend a lot of time together. It was often a long time between catch ups, but like any loyal friend, she always showed up when I needed her. When I made bad choices and did the wrong thing, she was there. When I broke the no running in the playground rule in year six, she was there. When I stole a packet of Tic-Tacs, influenced heavily by my desperation to fit in with my friends, she was there. When I kissed a girl in high school, she was there.

I didn't like being her friend. I didn't like her hanging around. She felt heavy and sludgy and yuck. She was like the annoying friend you just couldn't shake. So, you just had to accept it. You didn't have to like it. She was the obligatory friend. I was obliged to keep her in my life.

When I first considered that I wasn't happy in my marriage, I only got half-way through the first sentence in my head before I shut that crazy unacceptable story down. This was not a story that a good girl who always does the right thing would even contemplate. And just in case there was any doubt, or any further consideration that this could actually be my truth, shame burst in, with ferocity akin to King Kong's rescue of the damsel in distress, causing the destruction of any truth that lay in her way.

And so, life went on, day after day, week after week, doing all the doing things I did to band aid the realness within. It worked a treat. I was playing my good girl character so well. I was doing the right thing. The right thing by all the rules of what the right thing was, made by people I didn't even know. I was doing the right thing for them.

But here is the thing with your truth. The truth of who you are, that lies deep within your soul. Well, she gets to this stage in life when she kinda goes back to those bad words that my semi-Catholic family had long ago forbidden:

'Fuck this shit! I'm not doing this shit anymore.'

Drop The Act

I had found a kind of *fuck* within me that I hadn't known before. It came from a rumble deep down, somewhere I couldn't see, I couldn't hear, but I could feel. It was a realisation of knowing there was more. It was a feeling of wanting more. The rumble unsettled me. Something was calling me. I couldn't shut it down, I couldn't ignore it. I couldn't turn a blind eye anymore. The universe was speaking to me.

13

COINCIDENCE...OR NOT

———————— ◆◇◆ ————————

Irony: a literary technique, originally used in Greek tragedy, by which the full significance of a character's words or actions is clear to the audience or reader although, unknown to the character.[3]

Before I had children, Friday nights were hijacked by the touch football competition Vawdon Cup, a tournament run during the months of winter. Every Friday night, after work, we travelled to Penrith for a game that would kick off as late as 9.30pm. These late games in Penrith were the worst. The Kingsway is one of Sydney's largest touch football facilities, home to eighteen fields. Eighteen fields of open grassland where fog slowly crept in, obstructing the vision from one end of the field to the other. The cold was bitter and unforgiving, most notably evidenced by the mark of a handprint left firmly on a butt cheek by the slap of a desperate competitor. A handprint still visible at kick off time the following week.

It was 2005, July 29th to be exact. Mandy left her home with her slightly less than sober husband in the front passenger seat, their

Drop The Act

two kids strapped in the back of her conspicuous F250 truck and headed for the 7.30pm game. She had barely reached the outskirts of her hometown when she cursed as she remembered having left her jacket at home, her lapse in memory somewhat out of character. She hesitated, considered pushing on without it, but made the decision to return home and ensure her comfort for the cold night ahead.

Mandy never made it to that game. Her decision to return home found her F250 perfectly placed in the oncoming path of a newly licensed P plate driver fishtailing up the road, forcing her truck down an embankment, rolling over itself multiple times before coming to rest on the driver's side door. Mandy was trapped. Unbeknownst to her, the P plate driver, who narrowly escaped collision with her truck, continued on thereafter plunging head on into the car travelling behind her.

I believe everything happens for a reason. But I'm not sure Mandy or I, or anyone else we knew, believed much in the power of a higher force back then. This was a tragic accident, involving multiple innocent beings, who would be left with trauma for years to come. What could the greater purpose of this terrible tragedy possibly have been.

Mandy is a keen sportswoman accomplished in numerous different codes. But as a child, her sporting prowess was witnessed only by her younger brother, her only opponent, the only playing field being that of their backyard where after school they played round after round of tackle football. Mandy's fierce competitive streak knew no limit and was compromised for no one. Well actually that's not entirely true. As the game neared completion and they prepared to retire for the night, Mandy allowed Matt to score once and only once, and only when her score reached just shy of one hundred points.

On weekends, she sat and watched as her brother played competitively and she morphed from her brother's greatest competitor to his greatest fan.

In her years at Camden High School, Mandy spent as much time possible outside the classroom, on any sporting field, in any sporting event. Trips to Cowra for the annual inter-school sporting showcase were the highlight of her schooling days and was probably the thing that kept her in school for as long as it did. As soon as she was of legal age, she sat for her driver's license. The greatest gift of her newfound independence was her emergence into the world of competitive sport, outside of school.

Mandy was ruthless in her competitive spirit. It was win at all costs. She carried the weight of tremendous expectation, the expectation to perform and the expectation to win. And if you weren't on board with her, you were off the team. Mandy wasn't there to make friends. She wasn't concerned about making enemies. She was there for the medal, the shiny little gold disc that, when hung around her neck, spoke to her heart. *You are the winner. You are worthy.*

Mandy's fierce competitive nature combined with natural skill and athletic ability saw her accumulate a mountain of medals over the years after passing that test. One medal wasn't enough, nor was two or three or four. No sooner had she received the medal for one event, had she set her sights on the next. She was chasing something that couldn't be found within the shiny little gold discs.

Drop The Act

On that night in the July of 2005, Mandy's body was broken. Her neck and her back, broken. The surgeon left no room for hope.

'You will never play sport again.'

Mandy's days of competitive sport were over. The days, weeks, months that followed were the darkest of dark for Mandy. Her abundant collection of gold discs no longer spoke to her, they had nothing to say. What once served as a reminder of her value and her worth, no longer seemed to serve any worth at all. For what was the purpose of her life, what value did she have if there would be no more medals. No more shiny little discs to hang around her neck.

As I reflect on one of Mandy's most significant life stories, the irony is not lost on me. The irony that the very thing that gifted her the independence to chase her sporting dreams was also the very thing that had stripped it from her, in a split second, on that night in July 2005.

Seeing Mandy plunge deep into the darkness of despair was bitterly painful to watch. Even though we were only footy friends, it was the highly empathic gene I had inherited that allowed me to feel her pain, and the pain was agonising. For me it was second nature to offer help, to offer support, if for nothing else, but for her to know I was there. Nurturing people through tough times was almost certainly driven by my own search for worth. I rang, I offered to make meals, I bought her the Pretty Woman DVD, starring her favourite actress, Julia Roberts. The stories I told that once made her laugh, failed to generate any hint of emotion. I felt utterly helpless and questioned whether anything I offered actually helped her at all.

In the year following the accident, Mandy underwent surgery on her neck to address not only the pain, but deterioration of muscle in her right arm due to an impinged nerve. Sometime later, she underwent more surgery, two in fact, on the discs in her lower back. In my work as a psychologist, I had spent many hours with victims of motor vehicle accidents whom, after having suffered injuries half as severe as Mandy's had given up on life and sunk deep into a banal existence. But Mandy was not them. When advised by surgeons of the seriousness of her injuries and her subsequent fate in life, she listened. She listened very carefully to her own voice, a voice driven so fiercely by her desperate need for self-worth and self-value.

We all have an innate need to feel worthy. The need for worth will drive any human beyond any limit imposed by our thoughts and our fears. Mandy's fate would not be determined by the belief of anyone but herself. Not her surgeon nor any other medical specialist offering their reputable intellectual advice. What Mandy would do from here went beyond what her medical specialists' logical and intellectual brains could comprehend. She defied the odds and forged her own path, driven by resolute determination in her quest for a deeper sense of self-worth.

When I look back on my years of friendship with Mandy, someone who I thought I didn't like all that much when we first met, the significance of the motor vehicle accident that brought pain and suffering into her life, and also into mine to a much lesser degree, is not lost on me. Touch football had brought us together and offered a time and a space for us to meet. The accident, and the events that would subsequently follow, offered the opportunity for us to connect.

Drop The Act

More than a decade after the traumatic motor vehicle accident that put Oakdale on the map, Mario, an overweight middle-aged man carrying an energy of bitterness and resentment attended my office with his 12-year-old son. My calendar was closed to new clients, so I'm not sure how they slipped through, but here we were, nonetheless.

'I don't know what is wrong with him.' the exasperation evident in his tone.

He described a sense of immense hopelessness after countless failed efforts to help his son.

'We are ready to give him away,' he said after divulging complaints of his son's despicable behaviour.

His son sat on listening, unmoved by his father's words. I gave them Mandy's number and encouraged Mario to consider Bowen therapy for his son, who was clearly holding the emotion of an intense dynamic between he and his dad.

At his first appointment with Mandy, Mario sat watching whilst she worked on his son.

'Do you remember a car accident that happened here in Oakdale about 10 years ago?' he asked.

In that instance Mandy knew, she felt it. Images of the accident flashed back intruding on her conscious mind.

'You were the car behind me that got hit, weren't you?', Mandy stated.

In the conversations that followed it became clear that Mario, 10 years on, continued to carry bitterness and resentment from his experience of the accident. An energy that he held trapped in his physical body. An energy that oozed out of him like garlic sweat on an Italian grandfather the morning after a celebratory feast. An energy that was mirrored straight back to him by his 12-year-old son.

There are no coincidences in life. There are just people playing their part and crossing our paths for some greater reason, some greater purpose. It's not always apparent in the moment, and to be honest, it's usually really hard to see until we are blessed with the benefit of hindsight. But the flow in life comes with surrendering to the belief that we are always where we are meant to be.

14

ACHIEVEMENTS

―――――――――― ◆◇◆ ――――――――――

During my young adult life, netball was my sport. I earned a reputation as the zippy little centre with tenacious determination and was selected to play in Camden's representative team. No matter how many times I had taken the court wearing the bib with a large C emblazoned across my chest, or how many games we had successfully scored more goals than an equally determined opposition, the achievement of having been awarded the centre position at representative level, came as a genuine shock. And with an equally generous serving of disbelief.

'I can't believe they picked me.'

Excitement quickly turned to terror as the expectation I held of myself was brightly illuminated within, shining a light directly on my good friend imposter syndrome. Playing netball every Saturday at the local courts of Camden was one thing but having to travel outside our acceptable radius zone and compete against all the

Drop The Act

real netballers, the really good netballers, was a totally different ball game.

Mum was a die-hard netball fan, still competing at an age where we all played together in the same team and accumulated trophies, season after season. Of course, Mum would transport me to carnivals around the state, irrespective of the early morning wakeups and the distance required to travel. Her willingness to get out of bed well before the sun had even thought about making an appearance spoke volumes of her dedication to me and my pursuits in sport. She organised my uniform, she braided my thick fuzzy mop of hair and packed an esky full to the brim of both nutritious, and less than nutritious snacks that would sustain my energy through the day. Her trusty blue 7-seat Pajero clocked up kilometre after kilometre as she drove me, and half my teammates across the city to the relevant locations.

The excitement was evident in the nervous chatter and giggling whispers that filled the car, serving somewhat as a distraction of what lay ahead. On arrival at the carpark of the hosting association, the anxiety of anticipation flooded in despite the persistent chatter amongst the other girls. The anxiety, for me, was internally debilitating. I don't know what I looked like on the outside, but on the inside intense nausea fuelled by a sense of dread encompassed me. It was all too much, I just wanted to go home. But I never said that. I never said it out loud. I never spoke about how big these feelings were that took over my entire body. It was just normal for me. It was just who I was.

Playing the part of the good girl served me well, in some ways. The good girl, who would never in a million years ask her mum to take her home after having driven her across the countryside,

Achievements

pushed on and played each and every netball carnival. That good girl helped to put Camden Netball Association on the map after winning their first ever State Cup championship medal. That good girl, who would never tell her dad she was too afraid to get in the jellyfish swamped waters after he'd launched the boat in the pristine Jervis Bay, learnt to water-ski through fear-fuelled determination to hang on at all cost. That good girl who would never whinge and complain about the endless traversing across snow topped mountains in search of ski runs more challenging than Perisher's front valley, earnt herself a silver medal on the slopes.

Fear is a driving force. It has been a huge driving force for me in my life. Despite my fear I had earned myself countless ribbons and medals. But what was I so fearful of? Why was I so afraid of sport when I was clearly more than capable?

Earning more medals didn't help me heal fear. I was running. Running towards medals. But no matter how many medals I won, the pressure on earning the next medal was just the same.

Medals made me feel like I had achieved something. Like I was important, and I was valued. I might have been running towards medals, but I was running from my greatest fear. I was running from feeling insignificant, from feeling I was nothing.

15

SUPERPOWERS

———————— ◆◇◆ ————————

When Harry was born something opened inside of me. There's something about the love and the connection you have with your own biological child. I don't know if it starts at conception, or when your child is delivered and placed in your arms for the very first time, or maybe it's a slow gradual process that happens quietly in the background over the nine months of gestation. But when Harry made his grand entrance into the world, albeit brutal and somewhat traumatic for us both, it was like he came with a superpower. A superpower that made my heart grow bigger.

It is a hard feeling to describe. The experience of connecting to pure and unconditional love, is one that I think most of us experience for the very first time in our lives when we birth a child.

Harry's conception was the epitome of any good Catholic conception. Husband sneezes on wife, wife gets pregnant. *Wow, this making-a-baby thing is pretty easy,* I thought. *Just like in the movies!* I found myself unable to engage in the discussions of my friends when they talked about alternative yoga poses they had tried, after consummation, to try and fall pregnant. *It really wasn't hard at all.*

Three years down the track and the batteries to my biological clock had recharged themselves and filled me with an overwhelming desire for another child. My soul was calling for something greater, something more, something that I had found in Harry. I desperately wanted another child.

The universe must have had other plans for me, I guess. But I didn't want to know about it. I could feel the inner yearning screaming at me with a ferocity I could not ignore. And with that I decided that no matter what it took, no matter what lengths I had to go to, I was going to have another baby.

'What is wrong with me? I just want to have another baby,' I sobbed to my husband, the pain in my heart wrenching through my entire body after the tenth time I had taken the phone call from my IVF nurse, delivering the news of another failed cycle. I was beyond the yoga poses that my friends had previously encouraged one another to try. Early morning blood tests, morning needles, night-time needles, pessaries twice a day, internal ultrasounds with a sonographer from Year 10 science class, trigger injections in airport bathrooms, egg retrievals and embryo transfers. And then there is nothing else to do but wait. It was this space right here that was the best and the worst of it all. The waiting in a space of hope, of believing that this time could actually be the time. It is this space that obliterates the strain and stress of the IVF merry-go-round. It is this space that held me just above the layers of the soul-destroying disappointment that might come. I held on to hope.

Superpowers

Hope allowed me to believe that no matter what the cost, no matter how big the hurdle, I had it in me to keep going, to keep fighting for what I desperately wanted. And there was trust. I had to trust that whatever was meant for me, would come for me. But no matter how hard I tried, and how much I trusted, it was during each of the ten phone calls from my IVF nurse, in the very moment I answered the phone, that for a short moment in time, all hope was lost, and I abandoned my trust. I sat in the pit of deep devastation, a pain that isolated me and removed me from every human being around me. I was in a space so far removed from anything I had ever known that I knew so very well that I was there entirely alone.

In September 2012 I sat in the waiting room of a women's health clinic waiting to undergo the routine 7-week ultrasound that is considered 'normal' in the IVF world. The ongoing monitoring and checking and scanning that comes with IVF even after you get that phone call, the phone call where you expected you would feel a joy so tremendous that it would light the night sky.

'We just want to check and make sure....'

Check and make sure what! It felt like they expected this to fail. They checked and they monitored, and they watched as we all waited, with unspoken anticipation that it would fail.

'Imagine if there were two!', she said as she placed the cold wet doppler on the skin of my stomach.

I stared at a blank TV monitor, the screen as black as the space inside me. As the screen came to life, two white circles popped up, presenting themselves as clear as day. There were no words required. There they were. The two little beings who had chosen to come to me, in this moment, at this time. And in that moment, at that time, a little bit of light filled just a little bit of space on the inside of me.

Fear is a terrible thing. It tortures us over the many untruths we create in the stories of our mind. When I was pregnant with the twins, I continually visited the story that I could never love another child, let alone two more children, as much as I loved Harry. But when Jack and Charlie arrived, on the day after Harry's 5th birthday, they blessed me with their very own superpower and made my heart even bigger.

To birth a human that you have created and carried inside your womb for nine months is an absolute wonder. The connection with that child goes beyond any words that I can find for these pages. It is a soul connection. You give a little piece of your soul to them, and they give a little piece of their soul to you. It is the most powerful loving energy that most of us have ever experienced. It completely fills your heart space with unconditional love.

When I separated from my husband, I had finally learnt to put me first. I had found the belief that the upheaval of my world had come to steer me onto a path for my greater good. Not only for my greater good, but for the greater good of my husband and my three children. This was the path my soul had chosen for this life. This was the path their souls had chosen for their lives.

If there is any pain that will challenge your greatest beliefs, it is the pain of losing your children. The pain I found when I realised I would share only 50% of my children's lives from here on in, was tremendous. It was the hint of this pain coming that had kept me from stepping into my truth for a long time. I had birthed them, nurtured them, and loved them every day of their life, and now I would get to share only half of the days of their life.

I felt pain each time my kids left me. I felt pain when they wanted to be with their dad at times when they should have been with me. I felt pain when they were driven away for a week's holiday without me. But I never wanted them to feel pain. I never wanted them to feel the loss I felt when I didn't have them with me. I wanted them to have everything they needed to navigate through the challenges of a different shaped family. I tried to give them everything they needed. I was so consumed by what I wanted for everyone else. I hadn't even considered me.

I had lost faith in my choices, and I had lost faith in myself. But more than anything, I lost faith in my boys.

I lost faith in their choices. I lost faith in their journey in this life. I lost faith in who they are.

After the unpacking was done and the boxes were cleared, the excitement turned sour when I found myself alone. For the first time. In my new home. I sat on my verandah without a clue what to do. Willing myself not to cry. So instead, I wrote.

> Dear Harry, Jack, and Charlie,
>
> This morning as I sat in the silence of my new home without you here with me, I experienced one of the many waves of emotions that I have come to know since our family changed shape. These feelings are hard to describe, hard to put into words. They are painful emotions I have never known before.

Drop The Act

These emotions come with all these crazy stories that I make up in my head. Wild stories, make-believe child-like stories arguably more entertaining than any of the action packed spiderman series where Green Goblin (me) comes to destroy the city of peace (our once happy home).

I reflected on my pain and chose to look within, for what I have come to learn is that my pain is just that, it is my pain.

It is not your job to fill my cup. It is not your job to heal my pain. And although Jack, you believe from the bottom of your heart and the depth of your beautiful little soul that you truly are Spiderman with super Spidey-sense, it is not your job to rescue me.

I have come to learn that pain is a gift. A gift just as precious as that little blue box tied with a pretty white satin ribbon that I ask Santa for each Christmas…just maybe not as shiny or as pretty. To be honest, it usually feels more like sticking knitting needles in your eye but…I do believe that whatever is meant for me on my journey will come to me to help me heal the pain that I hold within, and to help me grow. The pain I feel when I sit in the space of being without you is the greatest gift for me, for it has led me to go within myself and find what I need to feel loved, to feel worthy and to feel whole.

Those that say we are broken are wrong. We are not broken. You are not broken. The 'perfect' life, the 'perfect' family, our 'perfect' world was left behind when I learnt that the 'perfect' mum was not who you needed me to be. I learnt that who you needed me to be was me. I learnt that what you needed me to be was brave and real and authentic and

Superpowers

true. I learnt to trust that who I am, me!....just me, is enough. I found myself.

I truly believe that your little souls chose me in this life for a reason. You chose me because somewhere deep inside, your beautiful innocent and pure souls also want to grow in this life.

When I see the hurt draw tears in your eyes and I feel pain flood into your heart, every part of my being wants to protect you. In some crazy-ass, Mumma-bear, self-sacrificial kind of way, I think that if I just feel it all with you then maybe I can take it away. But I know that it is not for me to rescue you either. My purpose in this life is to teach you to rescue yourself.

I will teach you to trust that whatever is meant for you will come to you to help you grow. I will teach you to trust that pain is a gift, an invitation sent from the universe offering you the chance to be brave, to be courageous and to face your fears. I will always hold the space for you to be seen and to be heard, not in spite of who you are, but for everything you are.

When you find the courage to look within, you will find everything you ever need. You will find your strengths. You will see your beauty. You will know your value. You will know your worth. You will find comfort in the love of your own heart. And maybe, just maybe, you will find your very own Spidey-sense.

You often ask me what super-power I would choose to have if I could choose any super-power in the whole wide world. And even though I tell you that I would choose to turn invisible so I can always win at hide and seek, I think that maybe I have already found my super-power.

Drop The Act

I will always be with you on this journey. I will walk with you when you can't see the way forward. I will hold you when you can't hold yourself. I will love you so big when your heart is open, and I will love you even bigger when your heart is closed. And when you find yourself lost, I will guide you back to yourself.

To have loved you every day of your life, to have held you in my arms and nurtured your precious hearts has by far been the easiest part of my privilege of being your mum. I know in my heart that you know you are loved. The greatest gift I can offer you is to show you how to love yourself. So I guess what they said really is true, 'Where there is great power there is great responsibility.'[4]

Love Mum xx

16

THE HOLES

———————— ◆◇◆ ————————

When you grow up in a family of five girls, there is little opportunity to develop any kind of only child syndrome. Nothing is sacred. Everything from clothes and makeup to university papers and boyfriends was shared. There is no such thing as a secret. No topic was off limits at the dinner table, or in the shower, or in the toilet.

I don't know how or when we developed this trait, the openness that has come to shock many family dinner guests over the years. Mum was not the most open of open mums. Her best efforts at imparting the essential knowledge for any young girl entering her formidable teen years was to leave copious supplies of feminine hygiene products displayed in the upstairs linen press. When the time came, we knew exactly where the necessary products were, and there was never any shortage. Mum was careful with her money, I guess she had to be with five girls, but she also loved a bargain. She was the kind of shopper who would spend 100 dollars to save 10. And so, she did, during one of her weekly outings to Franklin's grocery store. She came home with enough boxes of tampons to fill two shopping bags, and casually asked that I put them away in the upstairs linen press.

'Anyone would think they're going out of fashion,' I exclaimed, horrified at the sight of so many of these things. I knew what they were, but what to actually do with them was anyone's guess.

'Just try it,' my big sister said to me as she passed me a little white plastic thing that looked much like the chalk used on the blackboards at school.

'Well, it can't be that hard,' I thought to myself as I entered Mum's ensuite toilet, with my big sister waiting earnestly on the other side of the door.

After what could only be likened to an over-excited 15-year-old boys first experience with his penis and a real vagina, I exited the toilet, dumbfounded, and exclaimed, 'I have no idea where you put that thing.'

Over sharing was always the norm in the Glancey household. And to be honest, this hasn't changed much over the years. Under sharing was a whole other story. As I mentioned, no secret was ever safe between us girls. But as we got older and found ourselves in possession of certain information that best be withheld from all parental figures, the sister pact was born. These pacts were usually made out of pure necessity, rather than love, as two sisters, usually Emma and I, found ourselves with equally damning evidence against one another. We were both in the shit! In a desperate attempt to save ourselves, we put our creative heads together, and conjured up an entirely believable story that would account for every indiscretion, relieve each other of all responsibility and pass blame to some other poor unsuspecting teenager. The story was rehearsed, and we were set. Mum and Dad would never know.

'How did this happen?' Dad asked, pointing at the gaping hole in the wall outside of my bedroom. Our parents had just returned from a family camping trip with our younger siblings.

'Well, Kate and I were wrestling, and then I stumbled back and accidentally hit the wall with my elbow,' Emma said as we all stood looking at the gaping hole in the gyprock, situated somewhat higher than head height, let alone elbow height.

'Right,' said Dad! 'And you didn't have anyone else here in the house when we were away,' he said, more like a statement of sarcasm than a question.

'Nope,' Emma responded with great confidence.

'Wow, she IS good', I thought, as I was dying a slow death on the inside, totally panicked at the possibility that Dad might see through our story.

'Kate...?', he asked in a questioning tone that instantly, I knew meant defeat. He stared me down with intense ferocity like a gangster in a face off for a mere 2.3 seconds before I broke. I broke down sobbing.

'I can't lie,' I spat out, overcome with guilt, and subsequently blurted out all the incriminating details of our eventful weekend.

But that's the thing with sisters, forgiveness comes easy. Emma forgave me well and truly before the following weekend rolled

Drop The Act

around, and we started planning the next lot of shenanigans. But it was not until after a trip to Bunnings, a DIY patch and paint job on the wall, and a Def Leppard CD gifted to Dad as a peace offering, that Dad forgave us.

17

THE SYNDROME

The only kind of syndrome that you can catch in a family of five is 'middle child' syndrome.

Jess had found herself as the middlest of middle children. Not only was she the younger of two older sisters, but she was also the older of two younger sisters. Two younger sisters who, on their arrival had catapulted her into the space of no significance in the family. There is great intrigue and fascination that comes with twin babies. Blue eyed, blonde-haired twin baby girls were a stopping point for passers-by in the street as Mum pushed them around in a pram the size of a golf cart. Jess clung to the side of the pram, where not so long ago she had sat, and watched on as the Nannas of the town ogled over Amy and Beth. Jess had become un-seen.

By this time, I had already assumed the position of the good girl in the family. There was no point mimicking a part that I had already taken. Emma and Mum clashed; Emma challenged Mum and they

Drop The Act

fought. That part was already taken. Amy and Beth had stolen the limelight as the babies of the family. So, Jess found her own part.

By day, Jess developed the habit of whingeing and whining, a ploy she had discovered drew the attention of our mum.

'For God's sake, stop that bloody whingeing,' Mum would plead to no avail.

Other words of similar nature were directed at Jess and the constant noise she created in her determination to be seen.

'Would you just shuuuut up.'

But by night, when there was no noise left to be made, Jess retired to bed snuggled somewhere amongst the comfort of her seventeen dolls and teddy bears.

Armed with superior intelligence and a strong flair for creativity, Jess spent many weekends building forts with any bedsheet and blanket she could find. She draped sheets across chairs and used books to hold the corners in place. Jess found her own private little sanctuary for her and her seventeen inanimate friends. She guarded her sanctuary fiercely and we would all complain when she wouldn't let us in. It was her space, and she didn't want to share.

Jess didn't like sharing much. She guarded her possessions like a mamma bear guarded her cubs. They were more than possessions to her, they gave her something more. She had insane willpower that not only bewildered me but drove me nuts. Being the world's greatest chocolate fan proved nothing short of torturous as I would open the fridge, as late as October, only to see her savoured

The Syndrome

collection of colourful Easter eggs still sitting in a bowl marked 'Don't touch'. On more than one occasion the temptation would prove too much and I would scrupulously unwrap the delicate brightly coloured foil, nibble on the mouth-watering contents and carefully replace the foil, hoping to avoid exposure of my thieving ways. It never worked. Shrieks of outrage erupted from the kitchen on her discovery.

'Who ate my eggs?', she screamed.

More than 20 years later, my obsession with chocolate remained unchanged, as did her willingness to share. I broke into her house in a desperate search for her guaranteed chocolate stash. She was shocked.

'I don't know why you bother to hide it,' I said bemused.

Jess found a certain solitude underneath the bedsheets and blankets that she called her cubby house. But in search of further solitude, she masterminded her way to her own private holiday break at Nanny Glancey's house during each school break.

'And you're not allowed to come,' she insisted as she packed her bags, her seventeen friends and all remaining chocolate eggs. Off she went, on her own, in search of a time and space where she was seen.

Nanny Glancey was the sweetest little Nanny you could ever hope to have. She was the epitome of a Nanny, the embodiment of a guardian angel in the human flesh. She referred to all five of us as her little pet lambs. She baked homemade pies and bought us ice cream from the McDonald's located conveniently on the corner of her street. She loved to spoil us, not only with treats and trips to the shop, she spoiled us with her time and her love. She personified kindness and compassion, a being of love.

It came as no surprise as to why Jess found her escape there. But the more she escaped, the more she lost. The more she lost her connection with her sisters. Whilst Emma and I bonded over the creation of DIY projects for Dad, and Amy and Beth, well they were always Amy and Beth, zygotes split from the same cell, Jess was nowhere to be seen.

I've always had the worst memory. The number of times I found myself jump to my feet in a state of panic after hearing Mum's Pajero tear down the winding driveway of Berry Close, race out the laundry door and desperately gather the washing before she made her grand entrance, are endless. Finding day-old wet clothes in my washing machine is still a regular occurrence for me. But Jess had a memory like an elephant. When Jess finished school, she pursued a career in law. The combination of a highly intelligent mind together with fierce determination saw her earn herself the prestigious honour of having been one of a few young lawyers to pass the bar exams first time around. Adorned with the traditional wig and robes, Jess owned the title of Barrister.

Jess is a smart girl. In fact, she is intellectually brilliant. She has paved her way in life using her astute mind. She is a powerful being, a powerful creator. She has great passion for the things she wants. Material things. Houses, cars, and diamond rings. Chanel, Prada, and Gucci. Symbols of status, multiple degrees. She is the best at what she does. She has created all these things because that's how powerful she is.

But she has also created loss, disconnection, and isolation. Because that's how powerful she is. Because energetically, that's what she has always wanted.

18

EXPECTATIONS

———————— ◆◇◆ ————————

'How could he let me walk down the aisle and make those promises to me when he knew, he knew the whole time?' I said as the tears streamed down my face.

I was standing at my mum's kitchen bench after having made the decision to leave my first marriage. I felt like my heart was broken into pieces. Too many pieces to ever be able to piece back together.

I would love to be able to say, that after my first marriage failed, my faith in marriage was lost. But if I'm being honest, I don't think I had ever truly believed in marriage at all.

'I don't think we are ready; I don't think I am ready,' I said to him as we discussed the idea of getting married.

The conversation felt more like a stalling tactic than a true and honest commitment to my truth. I didn't want to get married, or

Drop The Act

I didn't want to marry him. But how could I ever say that to him. I couldn't even say it to myself. The thought of hurting him, breaking him, was breaking me, so I didn't. I didn't say it, I don't think I really even let myself think it at a conscious level. I just pushed it down to a space inside of me that I kept hidden under lock and key. And in that moment, I made a conscious decision to get ready. Make myself ready. I mean, what was wrong with me, seriously! He was a great guy.

'Just let me catch up,' I said to him.

At the Catholic club where I worked whilst studying my degree, there were two distinct hierarchical groups. There were the full timers, the smaller number of employees who were generally older and arguably more mature. And then there were the casuals, most of us university students, working a side gig to keep us from the depths of poverty whilst we studied. The full timers typically worked normal daylight hours whilst us casuals were there to fill the numbers needed for the more social operating hours of the club.

The boys in green worked back of house, in the cool rooms managing the beer lines and all things alcohol. There was only a small number of boys in green and they were a bit like a group of their own. They didn't work directly with the rest of us, they didn't intermingle shifts with the bar staff. They were a little removed, and a little mysterious.

My eyes met his for the first time, and a lightning bolt shot through me. *Who was he?* He was sitting at a bar table with the other boys in green, none of them wearing their work gear as they enjoyed a social drink together. His chocolate brown eyes struck me as they locked on mine, and my knees instantly felt weak.

Expectations

'Who is that?' I asked one of the other boys in green, in the most casual, I'm not at all interested, just wondering kind of way.

'Oh him,' he said. 'He likes you, and I can see why,' his reply revealing a hint of his own weak knee feeling, a hint that I very quickly erased from my conscious brain. *Those eyes!*

I'm pretty sure the universe was shining some kind of magical mystery light into those eyes in that moment, to draw me right in to where she wanted me to be. And draw me in she did! I can't explain the draw, or the pull, but the force was strong. The force of those mysterious eyes held me in that moment and held me for many moments to come. The force held me in the mystery of why he continued to look at me that way, when he had a fiancée. The force held me in the mystery of why his fiancée's car was parked at the front of his house late one night when I arrived to surprise him, even after he had taken back the promise of a life with her. The force held me in the mystery of why his car was parked overnight at the home of one of my co-workers. The force held me when I over-heard him whisper 'I wish you were here too,' on New Year's Eve into a mobile phone we shared as an engaged couple. The force held me when '69 girl', named according to her preferred position of activity amongst numerous club workers, called my home phone repeatedly. The force held me when I walked down the aisle.

I was naive to the universe back then and what she was trying to show me. I didn't see it. It's crazy to think, as a psychologist, working with these kind of people problems all day every day, that I could be so blind. But it wasn't that I was blind to what was happening, I was just blind to the greater purpose of this teacher in my life. I was blind to what he was trying to show me. He played

Drop The Act

his part really well, I have to give him that. He just kept playing it and playing it and playing it. But I still didn't see.

All I could see was that I was really bad at relationships. I could see that in every other area of my life, I had my shit together. I was a really nice person. I was a really nice psychologist. I was a really nice sister and a really nice friend. It was just within relationships that I seemed to experience the waves in my life. Like seriously, I was a really nice girlfriend and a really nice wife.

When I first met the brown eyed boy, I hadn't long come out of my first long term relationship. I had met him in similar circumstances too. Group of boy mates. In comes new boy. Mysterious eyes catch mine. Knees go weak etc etc. I was really nice to him too. I was really nice when he gave me his virginity and I was really nice when his friends thumped on the side of his car in celebration. I was really nice when he confessed that he had slept with one of our friends, and I was really nice when he started dating one of my closest friends right after breaking up with me.

I couldn't understand why this kept happening to me. *Why?* When I was such a nice person. Like really really nice, all of the time. Even in break-ups, I was really nice. I just couldn't understand. So, I just decided I was really bad at relationships.

I didn't know any better. And I don't wish that I had known it then. I don't wish for these things not to have happened to me. Because I no longer think that these things happened to me. I believe that all these things happened for me. I believe that she made those chocolate brown eyes sparkle, in that very moment, for me. I believe that the universe was guiding me to exactly where I needed to be.

Expectations

But why? Why has the universe sent me male after male, who faked it? Males who said all the right things, males who said they loved me, males who gave me just enough on the surface to let me think I was being loved. Because that was as much as I loved myself. On the surface. Fake. Nice. This was all I knew, this was the depth of love that I held within myself. I wasn't real! Being unconditionally nice in a desperate attempt to be loved isn't real. Being nice to the person who is breaking your heart isn't real. It is fake. And it is empty.

I do believe that my soul has chosen a path of growth in this life. Now, I can feel the pull deep in my soul, a yearning for true love and connection. Back then, I couldn't feel it. Or I didn't know what it was. Or I was oblivious. Or maybe all of that was true. But now, and only now, I understand why the universe sent me those great teachers. The teachers who signed up to play the part in helping me grow. The teachers gifted with the mysterious and mesmerising eyes, destined to cross my path in that very moment in time, to create the waves that would rock my perfectly fake little rowboat, gliding across the stillest waters. The sea beneath me needed to roar.

19

I MATTER TOO!

◆◇◆

When Simon and I moved on from the family home we built on one of the unspoiled acre blocks where I had spent my childhood, we each purchased our own home, five minutes drive from one another.

My new home, a direct reflection of my personality, and his new home, a direct reflection of his. Mine, a 60-year-old renovated cottage with hints of the era of its birth. His, a younger brick home renovated by the previous male owner, his masculinity ever present in the new modern touches and a garage sizeable enough to fit three cars, three motorbikes, eight push bikes and a man cave fit for bragging rights amongst all envious males, particularly the three young males I had birthed.

This was not the first time I had owned my own house, but it would be the first time my house would be my own home, just mine. Lavender linen bed sheets, soft pink bath towels and white timber floors spoke volumes of the theme I was embracing in my home. Roblox bedsheets, Minecraft doona covers and an explosion of

Drop The Act

Marvel paraphernalia spoke volumes of his. We had each found the space, within our own homes, to express a part of ourselves without the compromise necessary for a harmonious partnership. My home was mine. His home was his.

'When I'm at Dad's place, I get to be a boy's boy. And when I come to your place, I have to be a little bit gay,' Harry said, with a slight flick of the hand as he reflected on the new life he was forced to embrace. A life that still included one mum and one dad, but two different homes. He giggled as he said it, and I giggled too.

Harry is a funny kid. He is quick witted and smartly facetious. He has a sense of humour fit to entertain a crowd of not only his peers, but an audience well beyond his years. In his kindergarten class, during a very quiet and respectful lesson on religion, one of the children in the classroom let out a fart. A squeaky high-pitched expulsion of sound not unlike what could be heard coming from the music room of the junior school brass band. *Brrrrrrrrrrrrrr!* The class erupted into fits of uncontrollable laughter, leaving Mrs Lawless powerless to continue the lesson. Without hesitation, Harry stood at his desk and announced above the noise of 24 giggling children:

'Guys don't be slack, Mrs Lawless can't help it!'

The giggling continued, not at the expense of Mrs Lawless, but along with Mrs Lawless, as she too found herself in a state of uncontrollable laughter.

Humour is a trait that has spread widely through my family. Gezza always loved a good joke. His jokes were more like longwinded stories performed with unrestrained animation; jokes he was eager to tell anyone willing to listen. As kids, we heard Dad tell the same

I matter too!

jokes over and over, each of us rolling our eyes, trying not to laugh whilst he chuckled heartily as he delivered the perfect punch line. But as we got older, each of us developed our own way of expressing humour and the fight began. Who would be the funniest sister?

Betty told jokes in the lunchroom of Toys R Us to the team of minions she was there to inspire. Each Wednesday evening, we gathered for our weekly dinner at Dad's, and Betty would share the success, or more often failure at her attempt to deliver the punch line at the end of the joke rather than revealing it prematurely. She would rehearse a new joke with a plan to impress in the upcoming week.

Emma was funny without effort. Her ability to abuse the English language without awareness provided more than a few hilarious moments.

'A dead mouse just jumped out at me!' she screamed as she ran from the garage after fossicking through the animal feed.

'What's your favourite pastime Em?'
'Horse-riding,' she replied.
'But you don't ride horses?' I questioned.
'Yeah, but it's my favourite thing from the past.'

I was the master of self-deprecating humour. 'He says everything looks amazing down there,' I proudly announced after leaving the gyno's office following a routine post-surgery check-up. 'After all, it did take me three hours to prepare for our little catch up.'

So, each week, as we sat at the dinner table to share Gezza's speciality meal of chicken schnitzel, mashed potato, peas, and gravy we fought for the title of the funniest Glancey.

Drop The Act

It's not something you think much about when you first have children, but just like us girls eventually did to Gezza, my own kids started doing to me. Particularly Harry. He was fighting me for the title of the funniest. And he was good. He got me many times over with my own sense of humour served straight back in my face.

'Mum, tell everyone why you can't jump on the trampoline,' he announced in the circle of chattering mums at a 9-year old's birthday party.

'Hey Mum!' he yelled to me from the car as he and his dad drove away, leaving me standing on the steps of the hospital where I headed for one of those girly surgeries. 'Why don't you ask them to tighten it up while you're in there.' The little turd, he got me good!

But the thing with humour, is that it is a remarkable strategy for diverting away from any realness. Humour will soften the blow, eradicate an awkward vibe, and dismiss the realness in any real situation. Gezza was the master and his five apprentices had become masters themselves. So it was no wonder my child had adopted my humour and made it his own.

'So, I was just thinking about my birthday weekend.' Another thing Harry got from me! The ability to drag your birthday out to, at a minimum, a birthday weekend, if not a full birthday week. I could hear the tone in his voice, and I knew what was coming before he said another word. Trigger! Trigger! Trigger! He wanted to be with his dad for his whole birthday weekend. Well, that's what I heard anyway. Harry wanted to be in one home, at one place, preferably the boy home where farts and foul smells were celebrated and congratulated. But all I heard was, you don't matter.

I matter too!

What the actual fuck! I birthed you, you little turd. I ruined my perfect, well-manicured vagina for you, you little turd. I've given everything I had to you. Why don't you want to be with me, even for a little bit of time on your birthday, you little turd. The turmoil erupted in me like a volcano that lay dormant for a thousand years. A volcano that tourists visited regularly because it was safe and never expected to erupt. And here it was, that moment, like so many I had had before. The moment where pain shot deep into my heart. The moment where anger, sadness and despair rose swiftly to the surface….BUT the well tightened pressure valve had refused to let go. The moment where many times before, humour had very effectively dissolved the energy of my truth. The moment when I had used humour to eradicate a hard thing, a real thing. The moments where I put out to the world, 'I don't matter.'

'I matter here too,' I said, with strong conviction and a sound sense of self belief that I had not before delivered to my 14 year-old boy. I released my pressure valve, I let go. And in an instant, the energy shifted. Something let go in him too. I relieved Harry from playing his part on my journey of learning my truth. I relieved him of the weight he carried in holding that mirror right in my face. The mirror back to me, for me to see what I was putting out into the universe. The lack of value in myself, the lack of belief in myself, the belief that I didn't matter. He had been holding this mirror for long enough, and it was time for me to own my shit. He hadn't been doing this to me, he was doing this for me.

20

REVOLVING DOORS

———————— ◆◇◆ ————————

When one door closes, another one opens…so they say. Or maybe they should say, a new door won't open, until you close this one!

When Jess left, she left a massive gaping hole in my life, and in my heart. Not only did Jess leave, but she left with her husband, the only man I had ever felt a brother like connection with. She left with my niece, the only little girl I had ever felt a daughter like connection with. And she left with my two nephews. I didn't know a life without Jess. She had been my side kick, my wing man for like, ever. I was her maid of honour, and she was mine. We navigated the journey of IVF together. We shared in the triumphs and grieved through the failures. I had witnessed each of her children's first breath and she had witnessed each of mine. It was a hole I didn't want to fill, well not with anyone else anyway. I just filled it myself. Like a hole I'd dug for a new tree, but then changed my mind and just filled it back in. I just closed it over. I put on a smile. And decided I didn't need it filled. I was okay.

Drop The Act

'Do you want me to come and help you with the garden?', Mandy asked with an energy that I could feel. An energy that she wanted to give. To help.

'No thanks, I'm okay,' I lied. I only had 30 rose bushes to plant, 300 hedges to trim and 10 tonnes of mulch to shovel. I didn't need anyone to help me, I didn't need to rely on anyone.

'Are you sure, I'm happy to come and help?' She pushed, gently and genuinely.

'No thanks, I'm good'.

I was totally okay doing all the life things, all by myself. I had a husband, who was always around, when his more than demanding corporate role allowed, and my three amazing boys, who I loved with everything I was. And that's all I needed.

Mandy and I had been friends for more than two decades. She was a good friend, sometimes. We shared a lot of great times together. We played football together, we played soccer together. We shared great triumphs and great sorrows together. We travelled near and far, representing our local club, our state, and our country. We were great sport friends.

When I heard Mandy refer to me as one of her best friends, I was shocked and confused. I kind of thought we were just footy friends. I mean, we did socialise together at times, but most often it was sport and sporty functions. We always had a lot of fun together when we did socialise, we were a great pair. I was funny, and she laughed at me. Like, all the time! So, we worked.

Revolving doors

Mandy is an all or nothing kind of person. When she gives, she gives 250%. Whether it be her sport, her work, her friendships, or her relationships. She has a massive heart, and she gives so much so willingly to anyone or anything that matters to her. I had enjoyed moments throughout our longstanding friendship when I was on the receiving end of Mandy's giving. When we were away for a tournament, she gave me her socks when I forgot my own. She made me breakfast when I failed to consider that I may need sustenance on day one of a three-day tournament. She strapped my ankles when I'd given away my own roll of tape. She bought my lunch when I was too busy talking to get to the canteen, and she called my mobile to get me to the appropriate field on time. Until she found a new partner. A new someone in her life who was now on the receiving end of her giving. And then it all stopped. Just like that, her 250% went to someone else, and I was alone. Again! I was all alone again. It would have been nice if she had eased back to 50/50, or 80/20 even, but no. It was like going from all to nothing. There I was, at tournaments with no food, no strapping tape for my dodgy ankles and late to every game. The girls all laughed at me, and I laughed at me too.

'She's so airy fairy,' Mandy laughed, whilst rolling her eyes.

At least I brought my own socks this time I thought. *That's right, I don't need you. If you don't need me then I don't need you.* And I closed that hole too.

So, no! I don't need your help with my ridiculously huge garden. I don't need you. I had shut that hole and I wasn't prepared to open it again. I had experienced the 250%, and I had experienced the nothing. And the nothing sucked, it hurt. It really hurt. It made me feel like I was disposable to her, like I was nothing. Like in any

Drop The Act

moment, when a shiny new toy came along, I wasn't needed anymore.

I don't know how it came about, or what came over me. Maybe it was Mandy's persistent ways, but there she was, digging holes in my garden and shovelling the mountain of mulch sizeable enough to block all access in and out of my property. Maybe it was out of sheer desperation to end the daily trek up and down the driveway armed with three kid's school bags, or the pain of my blistering hands that erupted after only three wheelbarrow loads of mulch, but at some stage I said yes.

'I thought you and Jess were close. It was like you never had time for anyone else because you were always with her.' Fuck! The door opened.

21

BETRAYAL

———————— ◆◇◆ ————————

'I could do cartwheels down my hallway, and I don't think Simon would even bat an eyelid,' I let slip from my mouth in a weak moment of truth.

'What!', Mandy said, 'You guys have the perfect relationship.'

Yeah, you're right, I thought, part of me wishing I could take back the little snippet of disclosure of my personal life, and part of me wanting to blurt out and share with someone the hidden secrets of my desperate sadness within my marriage.

Yeah, you're right! I do have the perfect marriage. I have the perfect husband, three perfect little boys, the perfect dream home, and an all-round perfect life. So why did I feel this desperate need to share the feeling I held so deep and so hidden. The feeling of something lacking.

I thought I had everything I wanted. I had a great husband. Simon was kind, caring and considerate. He kissed me goodbye in the morning, when I saw him, and kissed me hello when he returned home at night just in time to tuck the boys into bed. He is an amazing dad. Always attentive to the boys, eager to read bedtime story books or tell make believe stories where Harry, Jack and Charlie featured as the heroes rescuing innocent victims from the evil ways of a corrupt villain. I loved watching their little faces light up in delight as they listened and waited to hear how the story would unfold, and who would get to be the hero that saved the day. They loved his stories and they loved him. They loved every moment he lay awake with them, and every moment he lay sleeping with them.

I loved that for them too. I loved the connection they shared and the memories they collected in those moments. In that time when he gave all of himself to them.

Marriage, two professional careers, two sporting careers and three children was not an easy juggle. The demands were real. In life, I believe we are all just doing our best. I believe we tried our best at balancing the seesaw that was our life. Me on one end, him on the other, and all the life things in between. But there is only so much you can fit on your own family seesaw, only so much you are willing to try and balance. And sometimes the weight of one end feels heavy, too heavy to lift. But a true team player doesn't just get off the seesaw. You can't just jump off and leave the other end to fall in a crashing heap.

I never had anything bad to say about Simon. On so many occasions, over so many girls-only dinners, I listened to my girlfriends complain about their husband's frustrating ways. How their husband had switched off his phone after arriving at the pub to avoid his wife's attempts at summoning him home after he'd reached a more than reasonable curfew. How their husband had stumbled home drunk after bashing on the neighbour's front door so intoxicated that he'd mistaken the neighbour's house for his own. How their husband had turned their garage into an open invitation man cave for the neighbours in the street to watch the footy every weekend and sink enough bottles of beer to welcome the sunrise the following morning. I never had anything to contribute to these conversations. Simon never did those things. He didn't drink often, he didn't frequent the pubs, he never switched off his phone. I really did have the perfect husband.

Each and every time I found myself visiting that feeling of lacking, the feeling of yearning for something more, I found myself feeling selfish and needy. I must have been high maintenance. What more could I have asked for? What more could I want?

I buried that yearning for a long time. I kept it hidden from my family. I kept it hidden from my friends. I tried to keep it hidden from myself. Simon was doing his best, and to complain or denigrate him for his efforts within our family felt like a betrayal. A betrayal to him. So, I continued to hide, and I continued to betray myself.

When I first met Mandy, she mowed lawns for a living. She ran the service department of her family-owned business. She trimmed all the hedges on her 60-acre property. She cut wood for fun. She lifted heavier than most males in the gym. And of course, she played sport. She was the manliest woman I knew.

Mandy's soul had chosen a tough path. She chose a life, born and raised in a small country town, to two parents devoted to the hard work of the land just as passionately as their devotion to the town in which they lived, and the small minds that are too often found in

Drop The Act

multi-generational communities. Living in an abusive relationship was the preferred option to leaving. Leaving would have people talk. And people talking was not okay. Not by any means.

'Do you think I should leave?', she asked me one morning on the trip home from touch football training in her F250 truck.

'I think you deserve to be happy,' I replied knowing full well the enormity of the advice I was passing on. She did leave. And at that time, I don't think she was looking for more. I think she was just looking to survive.

I turned up to my first game of soccer. I was shit nervous. I had never played a game of sport where you weren't allowed to use your hands. But I agreed to play, reluctantly, after Mandy's insistence that I would be fine. On arrival she introduced me to blondie. Blondie was Mandy's new friend. Her kids attended the school where Mandy lived. She was just another mum who had decided to find themselves again after having kids and get back into some sort of life activity. When I look back, I mustn't have been too nervous. Not nervous enough to have distracted me from the thing I saw between Mandy and blondie. The energy that existed in the space between them. An energy that you couldn't see but could feel.

Five years later, whilst cutting it up on the dance floor with Mandy, blondie and a few other friends, and after as many beverages needed to have lost my guard and found my Dutch courage, I shuffled my way across the dance floor, leaned into the ear of an unsuspecting friend and shouted above the music:

'You know, if you and Mandy were a little bit more than friends, I would never think anything different of you.'

Betrayal

There it was. It was out there. For real, in real words, in real life. A knowing that I had felt for many of the years they lived trapped beneath the truth of a love, a love so deep and so magnetic that not even the threat of ostracism and abandonment could polarise. And somewhere between the words leaving my mouth and reaching her soul, something was unlocked.

The pain of moving her truth from inside Pandora's box out into real life was nothing short of tremendous. A pain that by comparison, saw the departure from her marriage pale into insignificance. She showed up and braved the big wide world and found herself standing completely alone. She found herself in the most broken of broken places, a place that made standing alone seem too big and too hard and too scary. A place that made her believe there surely was somewhere better to be than here on this earth.

When you hit the bottom, there are only two choices. To give up or to fight. And Mandy was a fighter. And despite many moments of pondering life's options on cliff top edges, she fought. She fought for her, she fought for her truth.

I've heard her say many times, 'Who would choose this life?' But she did. She chose this life, and she chose the challenges that have come her way. The challenges that have seen her forge her way towards her truth. To live a real and authentic life.

'Do you want to be real?', she asked me.

I didn't want to betray my husband. I didn't want to talk badly of him, or of our marriage. I didn't want to bring any of that deep yearning to the surface. I didn't want to face my truth.

Drop The Act

But I must have wanted something. Or not wanted something. I know I didn't want to betray him or our life together, but more than that, I didn't want to betray myself any longer.

22

CONNECTION WITH SPIRIT

———————————— ◆◇◆ ————————————

Mandy was a doer, and was always prepared to dive in, headfirst, with any new thing that took her interest. At times I felt like I couldn't keep up with what I joked, was the craziness of her new ways. It may only have been a week between catch ups, and she would have had a new garden built or a room in her house painted and remodelled. She lived life at a fast pace, and nothing slowed her down once she found the energy for something new.

'Oh my god, what are you up to now?'

Mandy met Wes, a very good-looking Swede who had found her coincidentally, if there ever is such a thing, through her work as a Bowen therapist. For Mandy, running the family business had become effortless and less than challenging, and in her quest for more she was drawn to study, for the first time in her life. With a long history of sports injuries and having volunteered as the football club's sports trainer for more than twenty years, she was more than suited to a profession in injury management. She had found something that aligned with her purpose.

It was around this time, in her early days as a Bowen therapist that Mandy had also found herself fighting to find her truth in her personal life.

In 2010 Simon, Mandy and I all travelled to New Zealand to play Oz tag at the Trans-Tasman tournament. A team selected from a number of other teams who had competed at the Australian Nationals. It was on this tour that we met Dave.

Dave was a great guy. A fit healthy young man with a zest for life. We spent weeks training together in the lead up to the tournament, and then a week together on tour.

There is something unique that happens when strangers come together in a team environment with the drive of a common goal. Unique friendships are formed. Bonds are created that last a lifetime.

The weeks following a tournament are often tough. The extraordinary highs that come with such great accomplishments leaves you feeling extraordinary lows when you return to the realness of everyday life. But the weeks following this tournament included exceptional lows.

Only four weeks after having farewelled our teammates at Sydney International airport, fifteen of the sixteen of us gathered in an inner-city church to farewell Dave. Dave had been cycling on one of Sydney's major motorways with a group of friends, including students from the high school where he taught mathematics and sports studies. Dave rode on the outside of the pack, placing himself between his students and the motor vehicles travelling at more than 100 kilometres per hour. Without warning, Dave was struck, and killed instantly.

'Dave has a message he wants me to send his wife,' Mandy told me. Uncertainty and doubt were evident in her tone.

Mandy had found a path of spirituality on her journey of healing, a path that saw her investigate her intuitive and psychic abilities.

'Oh my God!', I said. A mixture of both doubt and intrigue swirling within me, as I struggled to combine the picture of a friend who once mowed lawns for a living and a friend who now embraced her spirituality and studied the laws of energy. I had christened her, *my crazy spiritual friend*.

At the risk of sounding purely and utterly crazy, Mandy courageously contacted Dave's wife and passed on his message, the details of which, she said, were unbelievably accurate and mind blowing. Details down to the love notes he carved into their tub of butter before he left for work, despite knowing that, destroying the perfectly set butter drove her crazy.

That is something I have always admired about Mandy. Her radical belief in what she does and what she knows, no matter how crazy it may look or sound to anyone else.

When Dave came to Mandy, not only did he come with a message for his beloved wife whom he had left here on this earth, he gifted Mandy the key that unlocked something inside of her that would shape her path tremendously.

Drop The Act

'So, Wes has taught me this thing called Rapé,' she informed me with a buzz of excitement that she couldn't hide.

'Oh my god, who is this Wes?' Mandy had a way of going through people. She jumped head on into anything and anyone new, and just as fast she would jump out. And like many times before, I sat listening to her divulge all the amazing details about this new person and this new thing.

'What the actual fuck!', I said as she blew my mind with the details of what Rapé involved.

'What do you mean you *snuff* it up your nose,' I exclaimed in sheer horror, as she laughed at my reaction whilst trying to convey the enormity of this new thing she had discovered.

'Is this even legal? 'Ummm, send me a photo of this Wes,' I said, with a questioning tone of who he was and what he had done with my friend.

Wes is fucking hot! Like super model, make money from the vessel you were gifted kind of hot. Not like anyone I'd ever seen at the local footy club where Mandy spent hours strapping men's athletic bodies. I could see why she would have tried anything Wes was offering. Just quietly, I would have tried anything Wes wanted to offer me too. But Wes wasn't drawn to me, he was drawn to Mandy. He was drawn to something he saw deep inside Mandy. Something more than she had ever seen in herself.

After googling, *Is Rapé legal In Australia? Can I get arrested if I do Rapé in Australia* and *Will Rapé kill me?* I decided, reluctantly, to try this crazy thing that she wanted to snuff up my nose. I'd never

Connection with Spirit

snuffed anything up my nose before. No snuffing, no snorting. I was the actual opposite of a rebel, and this was the most drug-like thing I'd ever been prepared to try in my life. Well, except maybe a puff or two of marijuana in my experimental years, but that's it. Other than my own moral compass, having a barrister as a sister only heightened my anxiety around illegal shenanigans. And besides I can't lie. I couldn't even lie to save Emma's ass when we were kids.

Rapé was nothing like snorting. It was not a white coloured powder, and contrary to my Dad's cynical opinion, it was not a hallucinogenic.

It was through my work with the plant medicine that I found the power to heal. To go within, to visit and embrace the pain of my past and to release myself from the characters I had played, the characters that had served me so well in coping with life's pain. But I didn't want to cope with life anymore. I wanted to grow.

Simon seemed excited for me. He listened to the stories I told of the experiences I felt as I did the work. The work on myself to heal. He listened, he asked questions and held space for me as I embraced my path of growth.

'I can feel myself growing, and I want you to grow with me,' I said to Simon, standing in the kitchen of our dream home. I wanted this for him. I wanted this for us.

But the thing with personal growth is that you have to want it for yourself. Only you can do the work.

Growth happens gradually, slowly. It's like releasing layers bit by bit, inching forward one little step at a time. You can't see the

Drop The Act

growth, you can't see the gap that comes to exist between your old self and your new self, not until the gap is wide and profound.

The gap I created was big. The gap was profound. The gap between my old self, my old life and my old me. The gap between where I stood before, and where I found myself now. The gap between those I had loved before and those I loved now.

23

TRUST

———————— ◆◇◆ ————————

I knew Macie before I ever knew that I knew her.

Before Mandy and I had ever formed the bond of a friendship, back when I thought she was scary and intimidating, someone who was definitely not on my friend list, I ran into her in the busiest Woolworths in the Macarthur region. Located more than 20 kms from my home and hers, and with at least three Woolworths stores in between, I never shopped there, and neither did she. So it seemed, at the time, like quite the coincidence that we would cross paths in such a random place, at such a random time. She stood waiting in the queue, a full trolley in tow, and as we crossed paths, we exchanged a very brief hi!

The exchange seemed irrelevant, and without any great significance at that time, other than the basketball-shaped belly she attempted to hide, without success, under a khaki pair of men's sized overalls. It wasn't so much the exchange between Mandy and I that caught my attention, but the feeling I felt when I saw

Drop The Act

her belly. When I felt her belly. Her belly holding and nurturing the life of her first born.

Macie made her arrival here on this earth at a time when Mandy still hadn't made it to my friend list. I didn't know Macie as a new-born, I didn't hold her as a baby, I didn't see her walk her first steps. But at the time of my next coincidental crossing of paths with Mandy, this time in Coles, there sat, in the front of her trolley, a three-year-old whisky blonde haired little being, pale faced and freckled. She was the cutest little thing with an appearance likened to the typical Aussie kid starring in a Weet-bix commercial.

'Hi Macieeeee,' I said as I leant in towards her, intruding in on her space, blocking her from the comfort and safety existing between her and her mum. She coiled back, leant away, and dropped her face as if her physical body could shut her away from the vulnerable space and energy, she found herself in when disconnected from her mum.

'Don't be rude Macie, say hello!' her mum demanded, to which Macie did not respond. She did not reply. She did not say hello.

'That's ok,' I said cheerfully, dismissing her mum's demands as I attempted to shield Macie from the pain and discomfort of her own vulnerability. Her mum didn't see it, and Macie didn't understand it, but I felt it, and I could feel that Macie felt it too. She didn't want to be seen. She didn't want to be seen by anyone but her mum.

For as many hours of as many days as she could, over the years to follow, Macie remained happily tucked away, safely, and securely under the wing of her mum. A place where she found comfort, a place where she best avoided pain. A place where she was held and didn't have to be seen.

In her desperate attempt to connect and to feel loved, to feel the love of her safe person, Macie learnt to abandon herself. She abandoned the feminine white dresses and matching ballet flats. She abandoned the frill layered skirts that flared from her waist as she twirled in front of her bedroom mirror. She didn't want to be seen for who she was, she wanted to be seen for who she thought she needed to be.

Macie was just like her mum. She loved the land. She never shied away from hard work. She planted gardens and mowed lawns. She fixed fences and dug trenches. She chopped wood like a boss. They did everything together. They camped together. They rode horses together. They played football together.

Years of dedication to numerous sporting codes including soccer, swimming and football have seen her accumulate more medals and ribbons than what she could ever possibly display on the walls of the oversized homestead where she was born and raised. Her natural athletic prowess was more than evident in the successes and achievements she enjoyed so far.

But now, it is real. Right now, as I write these words today, Macie is preparing for the Country Rugby League Championships. Now, she has the opportunity to go big, to break free from the small-town local competitions where she has dominated. Where she has been seen for all the things she can do. Where she has been seen for the power of her shoulder charge. Where she has been seen playing off the hip of her football obsessed mother, scoring tries every time she steps on the field. Where she has been seen as Mandy's daughter.

Drop The Act

We sat in the front seats of my car, awaiting the start of her training session for her local rugby league team. A team where she dominated, where she was seen for her strength and her skill. She spoke of the challenges and all the frustrations that come with any local team sport. But as she spoke, I could see her, I could see straight through her. I saw that she wanted more. But she was trapped in her fear. She was trapped in the ego defined character of who she thought she was meant to be, and the ego driven doubts of who she imagined she could ever be. I could see that she couldn't see her. She had long forgotten five-year-old Macie, the Macie who changed her outfit seven times a day, despite her mum's bewilderment, to admire the beauty of her reflection in the mirror. The beauty of who she was, the beauty of everything she is.

A part of her wanted to break free, to forge forward on her own path. But she was stuck. She felt small.

'You are keeping yourself small,' I said to her, provoking the glare of her signature furrowed scowl accompanied by her also signature expression 'grrr', which I had long ago recognised was her way of acknowledging the truth, owning her shit, and sitting in her own vulnerability.

I looked her in the eye and I continued. Mace, it is time to release yourself from the expectations of who you think you need to be. It is time to quit playing the part of who you think everyone else wants you to be. YOU have to do the work Mace. Not the work on the field, the work on you. You have to release the layers of fear. You have to face the judgement you hold on yourself, and you have to dissolve your own sludge pit of shame. You have to step into your greatest vulnerabilities. And when you do the work, you

Trust

will find you. You will find your own beauty, you will find your own worth and you will find your own value. You will find the courage to be seen. You can't wait for the world to see you Mace, you have to show up for yourself first. You have to see you first. And then whatever is meant for you will come. You have to trust!

24

SCHMEMMITT!

———————— ◆◇◆ ————————

When you write a book about personal experiences people in your life start to ask the question, *Have you written about me yet?* Some ask with fear and trepidation, others ask with interest and curiosity, eager for the insight of how they might be seen in the eyes of another.

When I first considered telling my Dad I was writing a book, that weekend at Manyana where these pages were first created, my BFF imposter syndrome popped in for a visit. Well to be honest, she didn't just pop in…she barged in, unannounced with a vicious energy of fear and doubt. Unable to ignore the glaringly obvious message of the purpose of this book, I forced myself to show up.

'So Gezza, I'm writing a book,' I spat out, before I allowed myself to think my way out of this vulnerable moment. As my mentor, my leader, my guru on all things psychology I felt a great degree of uncertainty in taking a leap forward and pursuing my own thing. A thing signifying my own realness, my own thoughts, and my own beliefs. The words written here are not words I had learned from him in the twenty odd years of working under his wing, they were coming from me. From my own truth.

'Well, I hope you're not going to write about me,' he said, accompanied by that infamous chuckle, the one suggestive of his ability to amuse himself.

'I've got a lot to write about you', I said. 'But don't worry, I've changed your name to Schmezza, so no-one will ever know it's you!' I laughed at myself, a reflection of him in me.

Emmitt is Mandy's second born. Her only son. The only boy in the family. With the physical frame of a small giant, he is the only adult, or almost adult, who is forced to duck as he enters and leaves through the front entry of my home, narrowly missing the low-lying chandelier. His feet spill over the end of his queen-sized bed and his chest is as far as I can reach when he hugs me.

Emmitt holds a grand physical presence, and his energy can fill a room. It is not just his size that draws the remarks from many, wherever he goes. He is the epitome of the gentle giant; larger than large on the outside yet sensitive, soft, and gentle-hearted on the inside.

Emmitt is the cruisy one of the family. He goes with the flow and the flow seems to go with him. He always falls on his feet. And he is rarely knocked off course. He is content in his own space. He knows what he wants. He knows where he is going. He looks like he has it all. But it is not too far from the surface where both his greatest gift and greatest vulnerability lies. His heart.

Schmemmitt!

The ego is our greatest mechanism for self-protection. It is the story we stick to that protects us from our pain. It protects us from sitting in our truth and it protects us from connecting to our heart. It is a place where we can stay safe, creating a picture of who we want to be, of what will serve us well. And Emmitt knows this space. It is a space where his heart is safe, where the sensitivity often stays hidden.

And then there's Macie. Emmitt's connection with Macie is never more present than in the many moments of competitive play on the farm. You will often find them towing each other around the dam on a wakeboard led by the farm buggy or lifting one another in the excavator bucket high above the water whilst the other clings on, in competition to see who can hold on the longest. Whether it be face slaps for TikTok challenges or tackle practice for footy, Emmitt never wins. Not because he can't, but because he won't. His heart is too big. His soul is too soft.

Yet in other moments, Macie can drive him to the brink of internal destruction. Evidence of Macie's flamboyant meal creations left abandoned in the kitchen sink, and her taunting display of biscuit packets left empty in the pantry are just a few challenges that probe deeper than his surface. It is in these rare moments when his frustrations rise and his greatest vulnerability is exposed. He finds his voice and speaks out. Immediately his words are met with a sharp reply from his sister, a woman whose energy can eat him alive. His heart is hurt, it pounds in his chest, and he quickly sinks back into himself, finding a space of protection from the energy warfare for which he is ill-equipped. It is no wonder he remains unattached to any one female at this time in his life. His space is more than complete by the female he loves most.

Drop The Act

Conflict is not his friend. He doesn't start it, nor will he finish it. He chooses to stay in his own lane. But when Macie crosses into his, moments of conflict arise. His heart is hurt. His spirit deflates.

Whilst Emmitt and I could not be more different in our physical height and build, we are alike in our heart. After a moment of conflict in the house, between him and his sister, I see his pain. I see him shrink. I see him deflate. I don't have words, I just hug him. He hangs on for a moment longer than usual, or maybe even two. And I know, I am sure, that all he needs is to be seen and to be loved.

'So have you written about me yet?' He asks.
'I have,' I said.
'And what's my chapter called?'
'Schmemmitt,' I said, with a grin. He grinned back.
'Mad!'

25

IT'S NOT ABOUT YOU!

───────── ◆◇◆ ─────────

When Simon and I built the dream house, I thought I had found my forever home. I thought I had found our place, where our kids would build lifelong dreams in their years of youth, just as I had in mine. I dreamed of backyard shenanigans and free-spirited play on the blades of grass that were once labelled Berry Close. I dreamed of a place where roots were formed and memories were made that would forever serve as the home ground for our family, a place where the boys would return long after they found their own wings, and indulge in the nostalgia of a life well lived. I dreamed that we would grow old there.

The acres of Berry Close were located in the township of Camden, a place, that at the time, was considered a million miles from anywhere. A place in the middle of nowhere. Dad's friends told him he was crazy for moving to a place so far removed from the civilisation he had known. But this is where he built our home. This is where I drove our Yamaha DS80 straight into the front garden, crashing into a well-established clump of gardenias, narrowly saving me from an encounter with the front door. This is where I learnt to trot on the feisty Arab gelding as Dad ran beside him, holding his reins as I bounced around in the saddle, doing my best to conceal my fear from him and the horse. This is where we spent countless hours running up and down the hand laid pavers of the fibreglass pool yelling, 'Marco! Polo!', whilst Mum bashed on the kitchen window, yelling at us to keep the water in the pool. This is where we called home.

When Dad left Berry Close, it was like the heart and soul of the home left too. The gardens were never so tidy and the trees lining the winding asphalt driveway didn't bloom like they used to. By the time the double storey, red bricked building was demolished, the acres had been carved into six. The four kid bedrooms, each one facing another, left uninhabited, and the oversized cedar entry door rotting at the edges, a symbol of the nothingness that remained.

We watched as the monstrous mechanical beast ripped through the structure, the house foundations crumbling like pieces of a Jenga tower. In only a few short hours, the dust settled, and the roar of the bulldozer quietened, leaving little evidence of the dream built, other than a concrete slab retaining the imprints of five children's hands.

'You should buy the shit block,' Jess said out of nowhere.

Simon and I had only recently completed our first owner builder project, a modern single storey home in a newly established estate, only ten houses down from where she and Nugg, the builder husband, had whipped up a home in a remarkable twelve weeks. This wasn't the first time we had lived in such close proximity, in fact, this wasn't considered close at all compared to the neighbouring acreage we had recently occupied. But being married to the builder husband, and harbouring a deep seeded passion for design, stemming back to her days of building elaborate cubby houses, meant that their roots planted in any one place never grew too deep. No sooner had they finished one project, that another begun.

'What do you mean I should buy the shit block?' I questioned.

I was unable to decide whether I was offended or intrigued. Jess had a way of sneaking into my comfort zone and ruffling the feathers just enough to shine a light on the possibility of something new, something bigger, and something better. Even though I knew that the modern single storey home in the newly appointed residential estate was definitely not my forever home, I wasn't ready to look forward.

That fucken light! It wasn't the first time, and it wouldn't be the last. I knew her all too well, and I knew me too. I knew that it only took a glimpse of what could be, a glimpse of something great, a glimpse of something that once I had seen, I couldn't un-see.

We were still hanging hot-air balloon mobiles and mounting new-born photographs when we started consultations with an architect named Reggie. After hours of consultation and discussions around the non-negotiable features of the home, including raked ceilings, exposed beams and internal barn doors, Reggie presented a design highlighting the glorious backyard views of picturesque rolling hills and a eucalyptus tree as old as the ark. What once was considered the shit block of Berry Close, soon revealed itself as the hidden gem.

Drop The Act

We broke ground, foundations were laid, trusses were fixed. Week by week, slowly but surely, the dream, my dream, became my reality. It was everything and more.

'What do you mean you've bought the other six acres?'

Jess and her builder husband were on the move. They were done with the projects. They wanted stability, they wanted their forever home. The six acres of dirt that had been carved away from my hidden gem, separated only by a double rung timber fence would be the place they would call home.

You would never guess that our home and theirs was designed by the same architect and built by the same man, the builder husband. Raw salvaged materials replicating the feel of an unfinished New York warehouse versus traditional country interiors surrounding a black combustion fireplace instilling a welcoming warmth in the home. The style and feel of our homes could not be more different, yet our dreams could not be more aligned. Life on the land we called home, shared by two sisters, two husbands, five children combined and more to come.

Jess and I were inseparable. Other than my sporting engagements, which she regularly reminded me were a huge interruption to our weekend time, we shared all of our moments. We built homes together, we holidayed together, we shopped together. I knew her inside out, and she knew me. I knew the seats she booked for each Gold Class movie event, I knew that I sat in C so she could sit in D. I knew the meals we ordered and how each was to be shared, spooning the chocolate fudge brownie from the edges, never digging through the cake. I was the normal to her crazy. And we worked. We just worked.

It's not about you!

Until we didn't. Until one day, or one week or one month we just stopped working. We stopped booking Gold Class seats and we stopped sharing decadent desserts. We didn't holiday together, and we didn't shop together. There was no more of us. There was something else for Jess, but there was no more of us.

When we built our dream homes side by side, it was like we made an unspoken pact, a commitment to a long life together, two families as one. The feelings of bewilderment, over time, turned to abandonment, as every weekend, I watched her black Mercedes bus, almost large enough to carry her kids and mine, exit her garage and drive away up the winding driveway that we once had both called home. Without us.

'Do you want to catch up for Australia Day?' I asked, desperately hoping for an answer that would band aid my heart break and allow me to believe there was still room for me, for us, somewhere in their lives.

'I'm not sure what we're doing yet, but I'll let you know,' she replied, causing a wave of pain that I struggled to push down. I waited. Available. Refusing to make plans. Refusing to believe that the pain I felt was more than just an overreaction on my part. There was no response. There was no answer. There was no Australia Day.

It was that moment for me, that Australia Day, when I broke. I reached out and emotionally begged to be wanted, to be needed, and the pain of rejection broke me. I sat on the stairs of my dream home that together we had built, lay back on the floor and stared at the ceiling that builder husband had designed, overwhelmed by a lifelessness in my body.

Drop The Act

It wasn't the beginning of the end. It was the end that had been shown to me many months earlier, an ending that I didn't want to see. An ending I had refused to see. I had refused to see that the dream we had created, the dream I thought was forever, was not to be. The light she had shone my way, many times before, was no longer shining for me. But now I could see. I could no longer pretend to myself. I could no longer pretend that the gaping hole left raw like an open wound existed within me. I had no choice but to sit in this pain. I had no choice but to feel. Feelings of bitterness and anger driven by deep rejection and heart wrenching abandonment. I had to feel. And feel and feel and feel. I had to let go. Not of her, not of her family. I had to let go of the bitterness, the anger, the resentment. I had to learn to forgive and to love. Not to forgive Jess, and not to love Jess, but to forgive myself and to love myself. I had to forgive myself for abandoning me. I had to love myself instead of waiting for someone else to love me. In a time when I felt lost and alone, I had to find me.

26

ENERGY

———————— ◆◇◆ ————————

Energy is such a powerful force. It is ever present in our universe and in every living being. It is the vital life force that flows through the human body. Energy never rests, it is never still. It can neither be created nor destroyed. It is in a constant state of movement. It is constantly present.

Every thought, every feeling, every pattern of belief created from the human mind manifests itself in the physical body. This is energy. The energy vibrates in our body, through every tissue and cell, through our entire being.

Energy is a highly attractive force. Attraction is the energy flow, from one thing or one person to another. When energy flows freely through the body it pulls an energy of similar vibration into that energy field. This is the law of attraction. Like attracts like.

It is through our primal, creative energy that our deepest desires are found. The energy of what we truly want. These desires are the force of human life. It is the information flowing from our higher consciousness springing to life in a physical feeling, telling us that in this energy space, we are aligned with our true being. It is through the energy of these deep desires that we attract everything we truly want.

We are all divine beings. We can have everything we want in this life. But do we really know what our deep desires are.

It is through the conditioning of a human life, where we are taught to think and feel a certain way and to accept the rules of others about what is right and what is wrong, that we lose touch with our deepest desires.

When I was married, I wanted to be married. I wanted to have the 'perfect' family. I wanted life to be perfect for my kids. I wanted to be seen to have it all together, and to keep it all together.

What I didn't want to see, was my deep desire. My desire to feel a deep and connected love, my desire to be seen. And even though I didn't want to see that, it was there, stored in a place I thought was safe, in a box I could keep closed, in a place left untouched.

But here's the thing with energy. Energy is alive and constant and powerful. Conditioned thoughts and patterns of belief won't keep that shit at bay. You can't put a blindfold on energy. You can't mentally block it from your existence. It is constantly drawing to you what you deeply desire. Energy will always win. Somewhere, somehow energy will bring to you what you truly desire, whether you think that's what you want or not.

When I look back now, I can see the energy pull that has always been at play between Mandy and I. There has always been a magnetic force, a matching frequency that has drawn us together. Long ago, Mandy consciously found her deep desire to be loved and seen. Her energy attraction was consciously at play. Through her ego, she was manifesting a tall, dark handsome man to love her and see her. But there was always something missing. Her deepest desires remained unfulfilled.

I on the other hand was unconsciously manifesting and drawing to me what I wanted. Not what I thought I wanted, but what I truly desired. To be loved and seen.

There is only one moment in my life that I can say I have experienced a true and powerful out of body moment. A moment where the power of my own creation, my own manifesting from my deep desires came at me like a steam train. I can only describe the moment as a departure from my conscious body. It was like my body and mind had come loose and suddenly, without conscious awareness, I was located on the outside of myself. And that's when it happened. When my body left my mind and surrendered totally and unconditionally to what I had been manifesting and drawing towards me. To what I truly wanted, from the absolute depth of my deepest desires.

And then I kissed her.

Well, my body did anyway. I didn't. Not the 'I' that I thought I knew. Not the 'I' that lived by the rules of what was right and wrong. The explosion of intense exhilarating energy took over my entire physical body and threw it at her.

'No! Don't you dare kiss me!', she said. 'This will change everything.'

Drop The Act

But it was like I didn't hear her. My body didn't hear her. The magnetic energy force that had drawn us together couldn't give two shits about the words being spoken. My energy wasn't listening to her, and neither was hers. The energy of attraction was by far the most powerful force at play in that single defining moment in time.

And so, she surrendered. She was connected to her deepest desire, and I was connected to mine. It was like two stars collided. An explosion no less than a supernova, leaving in its wake a new universe. A universe where dreams and reality combine.

27

FUCK AGAIN!

---◆◇◆---

Fuck! Fuck! Fuck! What the actual fuck was that!

Kissing a girl was something I had thought about before. Something I had imagined. Something I was attracting without conscious awareness of what I was doing.

It was something I had discussed with Simon throughout our time together. I talked to him about the attraction I felt when I watched the intimate moments between two females in a movie, or on a television show. And it was something he was always open to hearing. Something I felt he was accepting of, and even attracted to. But it was something that was a hard no for me. I always thought it was just fantasy playing out in my mind, in my imagination. Something that fuelled an energy of desire. But that energy, the energy of intimate desire, I had always kept sacred for him. On a conscious level, I thought it was normal to fantasise and imagine. But deep down, I think I feared that if I went there, if I ever crossed that line from fantasy to reality, that everything between us would change.

Drop The Act

When I told Simon that I had fallen in love with Mandy, he wasn't shocked. He wasn't surprised. I do believe he was devastated at the thought of what this meant for us, but his words to me when I stood in front of him in a state of sheer terror, knowing that my truth would in some way break him, are words I will never forget.

'I wondered if that would ever happen!' His response to me was devastating.

'If you wondered that, why didn't you ever speak up? Why didn't you ever fight for me? Why didn't you show up for me? Why didn't you love me!'

I was in a state of absolute turmoil. Juggling the pain of losing a love that I had shared with someone for fifteen years whilst simultaneously finding a love in another was more than my heart could stand. I was an absolute mess. I was married. I was committed to my marriage. I had never looked outside my marriage for anything or anyone else. I had never broken my loyalty to my husband. He was my everything. I gave him everything I had.

But in that moment, I found something more. In that moment something inside me broke open and I had found something I had never felt before. This wasn't a fleeting moment of passion. It wasn't a moment of exploration and fun. Whether I liked it or not, I had found something within me that I desperately wanted to feel. I just didn't want to feel all the other feelings that came flooding in along with it.

I had never been one to put myself first. I thought about everyone else first. I worried about everyone else first. I buried my feelings to meet the needs of everyone else around me. I didn't know how to put myself first when putting myself first was sure to bring them heartache and pain. How could I do that? How could I do such an horrendous thing to the people I loved? To Simon, and to my children. *How could you do that Kate. You are such a terrible person.*

The guilt and shame that flooded into my existence wasn't new to me. These were not feelings that I hadn't felt before. They were feelings buried deep. Feelings that long ago, I had learnt to protect. I had developed the perfect character version of myself to keep these sludgy low vibrating emotions as far from my present experience as one could possibly imagine. Being such a nice person and living such a perfect life was the perfect role to play.

But in the pursuit of self-growth, I wanted to be real. I didn't want to fake it anymore. I didn't want to not see me anymore. I wanted to be real and true. Being there for everyone else first at the expense of your own needs is not being true. Burying your own feelings to nurture another is not true. Self-sacrifice and self-abandonment are not true. I wanted to put me first. I wanted to show up for myself.

But how do you show up for yourself when doing that very thing brings pain to another. I agonised and for a long time I stayed lost in my own turmoil.

The guilt and the shame had rushed from my depths and absolutely encompassed me. I was isolated and alone in my own internal darkness. On my side, in my eyes, the sun didn't seem to shine so bright anymore. The stars didn't light the night sky. My eyes no longer sparkled when I heard my children's laughter. The energy in my heart was black.

Drop The Act

I found myself sitting alone in my car outside the local Woolworths. I didn't really know why I was there. I didn't remember making the specific turns on the roads to get there. I didn't remember if I had stopped at the traffic lights on my way there. But there I was, in a space and a place alone. A place where I didn't have to smile for anyone else. I didn't have to hide. I didn't have to be anything for anyone. And there, in that underground carpark, hidden away from the world, I sobbed. My head dropped forward in surrender to the pain, and I sobbed. I sobbed and I sobbed.

I surrendered. I let myself go to the depths of my pain. I released the tightly wound screw on my own perfect pressure valve. I let myself visit the cliff edge of despair. And in that desperation, I asked for help. I asked out loud, I begged for God, for the universe, for something or someone to help me. To guide me. To show me the way.

28

LOYALTY

———————— ◆◇◆ ————————

Staring down the barrel of owning my truth and telling everyone I knew and loved that I had left my marriage and had fallen in love with Mandy was met with great fear and trepidation. There was nothing more I feared than judgement, rejection, and abandonment from the people I loved most.

On a warm summers evening, after having finished a game of Oz tag I parked my car on a quiet street, and in the dark of night I rang Betty. My voice shook as I forced the words from my mouth and told her of the shit-show that was now my life. Her first reaction was that of shock. I had hidden my pain so perfectly well that the news I was now willing to share had sent her brain into a spin. She tried her best to contain her bewilderment, but I could hear it in her voice. And I knew exactly why. I had been so clever at hiding.

In the ninety-minute-long conversation Betty listened as I shared with her the truth of me and my life. She was curious in her questioning in a bid to understand, in an attempt to wrap her mind around the enormity of what I shared. There was no judgement, just love and unconditional support. And when the phone call ended, a weight that I had carried in my own silence was temporarily lifted.

It had taken every ounce of courage I could muster to step into my vulnerability and say those words out loud. The words echoed in my head as I heard myself speak. And at that time, that was all the courage I had. So, in a less than courageous fashion, I composed a long-winded text message to each member of my family, hit send and swiftly turned my phone off allowing me to escape the heaviness of this reality.

When the status of a failed marriage becomes public, people suddenly become the expert on your life. People assume to know. They want to find fault, to attribute blame. And as much as I knew that this was their shit, it didn't help to ease the pain of judgement.

I could see the judgement in their face. I could hear it in their words, and even more so in their silence. A part of me wanted desperately to explain, to justify, to blame. The words Betty had shared in that phone call stayed with me and echoed in my mind when she said, 'Be careful to know the difference from those who want to know for themselves and those who want to know for you.' So, for the most part, I stayed silent. I didn't share the intimate details of my life. I didn't bitch and whinge and blame. I stood strong in the knowing that my truth was mine and Simon's truth was his.

There was nothing like falling in love with my best friend, who happens to be a woman, that would expose my great weakness, my tremendous fear of judgement. Judgement was delivered to me, to both of us like a knife to the heart. It was vicious and it cut deepest from the ones I loved most.

Loyalty

Being disowned. Being told that what I was doing was disgusting. Being told that they would not visit me in my home in the company of my partner. Being told I was not to do it in front of them. Being told that they were praying for me.

I still can't decide what is worse. Those who openly share their judgement and their disgust, or those who hide it and pretend. Those who stop calling, stop answering your messages. Those who look the other way when you are around. Those who quit the team because you are on it. Those who stop inviting you. Those who no longer show up.

Here I was, again, drowning in shame. The fierce judgement and harsh rejection from the people I loved was triggering my own fears, the judgement I held in myself. A mirror reflection of my willingness to abandon myself.

After a sweet victory on the football field my team gathered at the pub for a celebratory dinner. In the presence of my teammate's families and children, I was aware of the absence of mine. Hyper-aware of having lost 50% of my children's lives. And it still felt so wrong to be socialising with other people's children when I didn't have my own.

I sat with my dear friend's daughter, a soul who has brightened the lives of everyone around her. I have known her since birth and the connection I have with her soul goes beyond my words. She played on her mum's phone whilst I chatted amongst the team. She scrolled through photos of people we both knew and pointed each one out with elation, interrupting every conversation. Over the course of the evening, I juggled the demand of her attention with the attention of my friends. Until she pointed out, with immense

Drop The Act

excitement, whilst eagerly repeating my name, a photo of me. A photo of Mandy and me. In that moment, for me, time stood still. What seemed like minutes, was probably only seconds. But she had my full attention. And I was stopped dead in my tracks. My heartbeat stopped, literally. I had no words. I was stunned into silence. *How could she do this to me? How could she?*

The screenshot of a photo, taken from a social media page, a visual announcement of our union together, had been sent in a group text, by her to other people I also dearly loved. My heart shattered…on the inside. But on the outside, I sat across from her, smiled and continued to share the antics of a well-played game. I totally abandoned myself.

I lay in bed that night, staring at the ceiling, like the ceiling might offer me an answer as to why. The pain in my heart stabbed through me like a knife. The pit of my stomach rose, urging me to vomit. I wanted to cry, but I couldn't. It was like the pain robbed me of everything in my body.

I tried to reflect, to find some sense of understanding as to how she could do this, why would she do this. But I was looking in the wrong place. I was looking at her, and I needed to look at me. I had asked the universe for help, I had pleaded to God. Yet I wasn't listening. I had been sent the pain that I needed to heal. I had been sent the pain of judgement. The pain of abandonment. The pain of disloyalty. The pain of loss. This was my pain. She wasn't doing this to me, she was doing this for me. The energy of these painful emotions had come from my own beliefs, my own patterns of thought, my own view of myself. Her actions in that moment were just showing me what I held within, and this gift was my opportunity to heal.

Loyalty

In every life there are defining moments in time. This was one in mine. This moment, in this pain, forced me to show up for myself. It forced me to quit abandoning myself. It forced me to release the judgement I held within. It forced me to accept the loss of another before I would lose myself. It forced me to see, to really find the power in my pain. To see that through my greatest weaknesses I would find my greatest strengths.

29

PURPOSE

For five years, Mandy and I had been running wellness retreats, offering the lost souls of the world a place to come and gather to heal the pain and suffering of their life. Mandy's shamanic healing practices together with the psychology of my mind proved a powerful combination in healing work.

Twice a year, on the magnificent property of Elm Lodge, people gathered together in pursuit of their own growth.

Drawing from the teachings of Brené Brown I composed a session on the power of vulnerability. I created a circle, a ring, where I offered the space for every individual to show up for themselves and step into their greatest vulnerability. They were to choose to either sit in the 'cheap front row seats' of judgement or find the courage to get in the ring.

In every session I run, I stand true in the belief that I can only ever ask of them what I can first do myself. So, only months following my separation, I stood in the ring, stepped into my greatest vulnerability, and shared the truth of my wounds that remained tender and raw. My voice quivered and the tears ran down my cheeks. My emotion spilling over the surface.

Vulnerability is an intensely powerful emotion. It is to feel exposed, to feel naked and bare. It is terrifying.

Stepping into the ring in front of these brave souls and baring my raw truth birthed a power in me. Not only had I gifted myself a newly found strength, I had gifted each and every one of them the permission to find that strength within themselves.

In the midst of this emotionally charged gathering at Elm Lodge I grabbed one of a few spare moments to check my phone. I was surprised to see a message from Mum. Verbal expressions of love are not her forte, but it was like she knew this particular retreat was big for me.

Nanny Sue's demonstration of love is most certainly in her acts of giving. She lives her life dedicated to her girls and the tribe of grandchildren she has been gifted. Having five daughters means her schedule is most often filled by the needs of each of us. Whether it be baby-sitting duties whilst we each navigate our busy lives or assisting with the school run, without a doubt her priorities are clear. Her girls.

Perhaps it comes from her own experience in life, but if one thing is clear, it is that her greatest desire for us girls is nothing more than to be happy. Her text read:

'How fortunate I am to have such an amazing child as you to call my own. You have chosen a tough path and you amaze me at how strong you are. Your kindness and compassion towards everyone is exceptional. I love and support you and want only the best in life for you. I'm eternally grateful for you.'

At the conclusion of my group, after many tears shed, country singer song writer Jo Caseley, a dear friend came to me. She put her hand on my shoulder, looked me straight in the eye, and shared with me an offering of unconditional love and support. She told me she loved me, she was proud of me, and she admired my grace and my strength. She had seen something in me, something that moved something in her. In the moment of my greatest vulnerability, love and connection was found.

In the weeks following the retreat Jo told her own story. 'I've written you a song', she said. I'd never had a song written about me and I was eager to hear her words, the most touching is the verse that still brings tears to my eyes.

'We won't run, we shouldn't have to hide
What we feel inside, what feels right.
And our loved ones, who leave without a trace
They turn their back on love
But we will fight it out with grace.'

I have always loved the saying, 'Be so unapologetically yourself that you inspire others to do the same.' We are all here, with our own pain, living our own journey the best way we know how. We are all just doing the best we can. The decisions I was making in my life, the actions I was taking to move forward on my own path were shaking the foundations in the lives of many around me. Whilst some people I loved reacted from their own pain, the people one step removed were reacting too. But their reactions

Drop The Act

looked different, they felt different. They saw a strength in my work, they saw a strength in me. And they were inspired to change. They were inspired to learn. They were inspired to grow.

In a commitment to growth, you have everything to lose. Everything you have always known, everything you have always thought, everything you have always felt. As I grew, some who I had loved grew far. And those who were far grew near. I had everything to lose before I could find everything I would gain.

This is the path I had chosen for this life. A path to heal the pain and suffering I carried in my soul. I couldn't expect others to grow too. I had to respect that everyone here has each chosen their own path, and in turn is responsible for their own growth, as I am responsible for mine.

When I came to accept that my children also had chosen this path for their life, I understood my purpose here as their mum. I understood that the pain and suffering that had come into their world was their choice, their path that they had chosen to heal their own pain.

On a visit to Manyana in another school holiday break, I drove Harry to the basketball court, one of the few attractions in town.

'There is something I want to tell you,' I said.

'Am I in trouble?', he questioned with a look of anxious anticipation.

'No mate, you're not in trouble!' The relief washed over him.

'I want to tell you that I love Mandy,' I said.

Purpose

'You love Mandy, like love love Mandy?' he questioned.

'Yes', I giggled, 'Like love love Mandy!' He took a moment, pondered the information I had dumped in his lap, and replied,

'Sooooo, that means you're pansexual then!'

I laughed, out loud. And he laughed too.

'Well yes, I guess it does mean that I'm pansexual. How do you even know what pansexual means?', I questioned surprised, yet not surprised at the things that come out of his mouth.

'Mum, I know more than you think I know,' he stated ever so confidently.

I hadn't told Mandy that I was going to tell Harry on that day. It was a moment that just arose. A moment I had found with my first-born child, the child wise beyond his years.

'So, I hear you're crushing on my mum,' he exclaimed on his next meeting with Mandy. In true Mandy style, in the discomfort of her own embarrassment, her face went red, and she laughed. And in true Harry style, he laughed at the humorous discomfort he knew he had created. A skill he had perfected, much like his mum.

In front of Mandy, myself and my family, Harry stood proud and shared a speech he had spontaneously prepared, a speech declaring his pride for his mum, his pride in the mother I was to him, and his pride in the woman I was in this world. Another defining moment in time.

30

PURE

———————— ◆◇◆ ————————

Jack and Charlie are the purest little beings that walk this earth. Their love is immense. Their love is real.

They live in a safe warm bubble of love. Inside Jack's bubble is Charlie, and inside Charlie's bubble is Jack. They are like one, split in two. One is never far from the other. They laugh together. They play together. They sleep together. They live together.

From the comfort of their own little bubble, they offer the world enormous amounts of love. They radiate love from their being. They share endless amounts of love wherever they go. They are a blessing to the world, to the universe, to the greater consciousness of mankind.

Whilst their older brother has the wisdom of many lives lived, Jack and Charlie hold an innocence, a naivety of the first experience of life. They want for nothing. They make little by way of demand. They sit in a constant state of gratitude for the smallest things in life.

Drop The Act

'Thank you for working so hard and spending all of your money on the food for us to eat'.
'Thank you for driving us to school every morning even when you have a busy day'.
'Thank you for taking me to my guitar lesson. It was the best day of my life'.
'Thank you for being the best mum I have ever had'.

They are a source of pure light, in every day of my life.

They make jokes that only they understand. They converse in a language that only they know. They know the energy of the other. In each other, they are seen, and they are heard. Their greatest vulnerability lies within their greatest gift, the gift of one another.

Stepping outside the bubble in which they share together brings fear. It is the energy of aloneness that triggers their greatest vulnerability. The loss of that sacred space. For as long as I can remember, they have never tolerated the space of aloneness from the other.

On many a night I have woken to the pitter patter of footsteps coming swiftly down the hallway, followed by a delicate whispering plea to snuggle under the covers of my bed, apparently more comfortable than their own.

'I can't find Jack', whispered Charlie, as though I knew of his whereabouts. Within minutes, or more often seconds, the pitter patter of two other little feet nearing my bedroom could be heard.

'I can't find Charlie'. And within moments of the reuniting, slumber was again found, wrapped securely up in one another.

To encourage their individuality, their own sense of self, I have offered times to pursue activities on their own, separate from one another.

'What is Charlie doing?' is the response I'm sure to receive.

'Charlie is staying here. Would you like to come with me?' I offered. And however polite yet purely honest the response was always the same –

'No thank you!'

When I told Jack and Charlie that I loved Mandy, that Mandy was now my partner they found it difficult to understand.

'But you're married to Dad!' they questioned innocently.

Despite the fact that their dad and I no longer lived together, I had to remind them that we were separated. I had to remind them what separated meant. I had to try and explain to them what it meant to love someone like a friend and what it meant to love someone like a partner.

'So, Dad's not your boyfriend anymore?' they questioned.

'That's right, Dad's not my boyfriend anymore.'

'And so, Mandy's your girlfriend?', they questioned with naive curiosity.

'That's right, Mandy is my girlfriend.'

Drop The Act

'Ohhhhhhh, okay! So, who is going to be your husband?'

They may not understand all the complexities of the rules of adult life. Right now, they are naive to the rules of society, the judgemental rules of who and what you should be, who and what is right and wrong. But what they do know and what they do feel is that they are loved. And they love to be loved. They love to give love. They love to receive love. They love the love that I have for them. They love the love that Mandy has for them. They love the love bubble that has been born in my home. And how blessed they are to know no better.

31

EMPOWERMENT

———————— ◆◇◆ ————————

I totally understood that the news of the 'change in direction' of my personal life would come as a shock. For all my family and friends knew, I was happily married and living an absolute blissful existence.

When you find the courage to show up for yourself, in whatever way that looks for you, you attract the attention of many. And attract the attention of many, I did. Whilst many people in my life were triggered into their own pain and their own judgement, others were inspired. Inspired by a strength. A strength to stand for something. To stand in your own power, in your own truth. To just fucken stand!

Heidi is vivacious and vibrant. She is sprightly and speedy in her every move. She talks at the rate of knots, seemingly without breath and drives like a bat out of hell on speed. She is chaos on legs.

Heidi loves Mandy. She loves her like the sister she never had. Don't get me wrong, Heidi loves me too, but her connection with Mandy runs deep.

Drop The Act

They are a funny pair to watch. Mandy calls her on her shit, Heidi throws tantrums when confronted with her truth. They bicker like siblings. But Mandy is always there for Heidi. And Heidi is always there for her.

When the news of Mandy and I broke loose, everyone had something to say. Our life, our choice, our love was up for discussion and debate with many of the people around us. Some said it openly, some said it quietly. Some stayed neutral, in a removed yet comfortable space and some said so much in their deafening silence.

But not Heidi. Heidi was not one to stand down. Heidi stood in the face of criticism and fought back in the eyes of judgement. She spoke openly and honestly. She shut down judgement and challenged the shame. She stood for Mandy, and she stood for me. She stood for us when we couldn't stand for ourselves. She was courageous and bold in her feat to protect the ones closest to her heart.

Dad has always been supportive of the endeavours of each of his girls. No matter what we threw at him, he was there. There was always a knowing that no matter what, he would love us and accept what we had chosen, whether it be our careers or our choice in life partners. However, support didn't come without opinion. His level-headed, well considered opinion.

'I just want you to consider that you might be getting yourself into something that could be really messy to get out of,' he offered, with a balance of logic and reasoning.

I had engaged in these discussions with Dad before on numerous other topics. And before now, I had always been swayed to defer to the logic. Run with reasoning. Take the sensible path. Do the most right thing. But on this occasion, during this phone conversation, as I hustled my way through the shopping centre, I stayed strong in my truth. I knew, deep down, that none of this made logical sense. But I also knew, at a deeper and more profound level that it didn't need to make sense. I didn't want to go back to my brain, the thinking brain, the brain that had always kept me safe, and stable and certain. I had found a deeper level of knowing. A knowing from a new place. A knowing that I just knew.

'I do really appreciate your concerns, and I get it. I really do. But I'm in it now, and it's where I want to be.'

The energy of certainty and sureness flowed from my body through to his. And an understanding was shared. I don't know if he could wrap his head around it, but I do know that he felt something from me that was new.

In the January of 2021, Amy, Betty and Gezza celebrated the event of the year, according to them, at a fancy hoity-toity restaurant in Sydney's eastern suburbs. It was one of those restaurants that served really little meals on really big plates and wines that you sip and spit before committing to the bottle with a price tag equivalent to some people's weekly wage. Amy and Betty revelled not only in the dining experience, but the opportunity for a mini Insta shoot whilst adorned in carefully chosen designer outfits, the significance of which was totally lost on Gezza. He remained discreet in his less than impressed view of what he described as 'ridiculous bloody outfits', yet less discreet in his view on the choice of beer available, or more specifically, not available.

'What kind of bloody restaurant doesn't sell VB?', he complained when asked about the annual birthday bash.

Drop The Act

Over the course of lunch, Amy's foundations were rattled. Actually, I think it was probably Gezza's foundations that were a little rattled by the news of his forty-four-year-old daughter turning into a lesbian. He shared a viewpoint and defended the story. It was the thing Gezza did. He always saw both sides. But it was Gezza's rattle that triggered Amy. He triggered her deep beliefs and her values. He triggered her moral code.

'This is not acceptable in this family,' she belted out with great conviction and ferocious belief. 'I will not have it!'

What came from Amy over lunch that day came from a great strength within. A strength not only in support of her older sister, but a strength in support of all women. Of all individuals. Of all beings. A strength that she had long ago found in herself, a strength that served her purpose on this earth. A strength of empowerment, a strength of self. A strength that she owned. A strength that she shared.

In her place of occupation, where she serves as the Chief of Staff, Amy lives and breathes their philosophy of empowerment. *The standard you walk past is the standard you accept.* She was not willing to walk past. She was certainly not willing to accept. She dived in the ring, nothing gracious about it. She embraced the power of her greatest beliefs and she demanded she be heard.

The universal law of attraction says like attracts like. Birds of a feather flock together. When you step away from the characters you have always played, you step away from those wanting to stay in that space. You no longer serve them well. And when you step into your truth, you step closer to those already there. You step in to love, you step into connection.

32

MANDY

———————— ◆◇◆ ————————

She is the yin to my yang. She is the strength when I lose my own. She is the realness that I cannot escape.

When I found myself, I found what I wanted in this life. When I found my worth, I found what I deserved. When I found my own value, I found myself seen and I found myself heard. When I found truth in my heart, I found truth in hers. When I found everything I needed within myself, I found everything I wanted to share with another. I found her. I found Mandy.

For so many years, Mandy had been there. Sometimes in the background, sometimes in the foreground, and sometimes everywhere in between. For all the years of our knowing, we had shared a connection, a magnetic force of attraction that kept us bound together within each other's existence. A connection that was formed before the physical reality of this life. A connection from many lives before. A connection that served great purpose. A connection that would come to be in this life.

Drop The Act

To find everything you need within yourself is to heal. To heal the pain and the wounds carried from many lives previous. To flourish in your own skin, your own existence, and your own purpose. And to share that realness with another is nothing short of deserving.

Mandy is a great believer in herself, in her strength, in her own power. She shoots for the stars and treads forward with persistent tenacity. She is grounded to the earth and embodies the energy of ancient wisdom. She has the heart of a lion, courageous and brave. She loves big, she loves with her all. She knows her worth and believes in her power. She owns her own shit. And she makes me own mine.

I, on the other hand, embody contentment and joy. I bring life to her days. Fun to her heart. And laughter to her soul. I am the colour to her black and the pearl to her white.

When Mandy entered my family as more than just my friend, she stood in her own power, in her belief and her knowing that what she was bringing was pure and real. She was here, in this space with unconditional love. She was here to love me, to love Harry, to love Jack and to love Charlie.

And love me she did. Through the times when I thought the cracks were too great, she loved me. Through the times when I thought the pain was too much, she loved me. Through the times when I thought the sun would never shine, she loved me. Solid, steady, and unfaltering, she loved me.

What did I ever do to deserve her, to deserve this kind of love? A love so strong, so powerful, and so real. This I have thought many times over. But what I know, is that I could never have found this

Mandy

love in another if I had never found myself first. If I had never found what I deserve. If I had never found what I was worth. And when I found me, she found me too.

Another summer weekend getaway in Manyana, saw us again, accompanied by Amy and Phil, Betty and Deano.

'She is an absolute value add!', exclaimed Betty as Mandy towed the kids around the lake on Gezza's brand new boat, the replacement of the trusty egg-yolk yellow speedboat that had circled this same lake many times before.

'I feel like she really adds to our family brand,' she laughed, inferring the rainbow of colour symbolic of human diversity. 'We should totally get t-shirts made.'

On arrival back at the house we unloaded kids, dogs, and all paraphernalia necessary for an afternoon on the water. Mandy strategically parked the boat by the hose, a routine replayed many times over following expeditions on her own boat. A routine on which she insisted, despite Gezza's plea to avoid the trouble. We washed, we scrubbed until she was squeaky clean. The boat, that is! She was a pro on the water and had this boat thing down-pat, so much more so than all the other females and males in the house.

'I want to thank you!' Phil, of German descent and of thick German accent approached me with what I thought was an offering of gratitude for his children's delight at the day. Phil didn't talk shit, he didn't actually talk much at all. But when he did talk, it was often profound. I had nicknamed him MVP.

Drop The Act

(Insert thick German accent) 'It has been one dream of mine for forever to watch two lesbians wash a boat in their bikinis. I am very grateful for you.' Deano laughed his deep hearty laugh. He stepped towards me, in his sure and certain way, bent over, wrapped his long arms around me and held me tight in a warm and affectionate embrace and said simply, 'I love you Katie.' An absolute perfect expression of unconditional acceptance and love.

'Do you want to keep sleeping?' She whispered softly enough to exclude herself from blame for dragging me from my much-loved slumber.

'Well, I'm awake now,' I smirked, hearing the glimmer of hope in her question.

It was still in the fives. An unreasonably early time to rise from sleep on a non-working day. I stood at the door of the bedroom that led to the balcony overlooking the waters of the Pacific Ocean. The view was expansive and stretched as far as the eye could see. The blue of the water was deep. The movement of the water calm. It was as though the ocean lay sleeping whilst waiting for day to break. I felt myself gasp on the inside, and the only thing that came out was 'Wow'. The rays of the sun peaking just above the horizon, casting a myriad of colour through the low-lying clouds. The most delicious sherbet sky I had ever laid eyes on.

'Life with you is just the best,' she said as she held me close, wrapped tight in her arms and kissed my forehead. 'I want to do every day with you.'

'Every day?', I smirked and giggled as if encouraging her to carefully consider her proposition.

'Every day,' she said, without hesitation.

'I want to do every day with you too.'

ABOUT THE AUTHOR

Kate Glancey is a well sought-after Psychologist in the Macarthur Region of South-West Sydney. She has more than 24 years' experience in private practice where she has worked alongside her father in their jointly owned private practice.

She lives in the historical rural town of Camden where she was raised, with her three boys Harry Jack and Charlie, and Howard the Labradoodle.

Her passion for sport earnt her a place on the Australian Oz Tag team and she is still kickin' butt on the league-tag field. She prides herself on outrunning her 14-year-old son on the footy field and the ski slopes.

Her creative energy is expressed through intuitive art. Her energetic fun-loving approach to life combined with her infectious sense of humour make her someone you want to be around.

Together, Kate and Mandy started Elm Lodge Wellness where they run healing retreats on the 110 acre Elm Lodge property in the country town of Oakdale in New South Wales. They have since established The Holistic Healing Academy and have expanded

Drop The Act

their work to include online courses and in-person retreats across the country including the Australian Whitsunday islands. They are passionate in supporting individuals on their spiritual, mental and emotional journey of growth.

Her previous writings have been published alongside fellow Australian author Steve Matthews and in the Amazon Best Seller *Letters to My Son,* Laura Elizabeth of Maven Press, and Drop the Act is her first book.

MORE OF WHAT PEOPLE ARE SAYING

─────────── ◆◇◆ ───────────

'I can't imagine how I would actually be here today without Kate. She is one of the most beautiful souls I've ever met and I'm eternally grateful my path crossed hers.

Rebecca Ekin

'Being so cheeky and 'real' makes it easy to connect with Kate. An absolute gem'.

Deb Hatcher

'A little ray of sunshine'.

Mandy Hosie

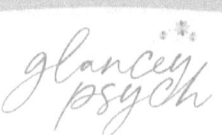

PERSONAL WELLNESS CHECKLIST

PHYSICAL	YES	NO
I feel strong in my physical body	☐	☐
I am free from pain and niggles in my body	☐	☐
I eat the right foods and feel my body is nourished and energised	☐	☐
I maintain a desirable weight	☐	☐
I get enough sleep each night and wake feeling refreshed and energised	☐	☐

EMOTIONAL	YES	NO
I recognise the stressors in my life and have effective ways to reduce those stressors	☐	☐
I always accept responsibility for my actions	☐	☐
I am able to prioritise myself above all others	☐	☐
I set healthy boundaries in all areas of my life	☐	☐
I can express my emotions openly and honestly	☐	☐

OCCUPATIONAL	YES	NO
I balance work with play	☐	☐
I enjoy the work I do and feel fulfilled in my current work role	☐	☐
I enjoy any opportunity to learn new skills	☐	☐
I set healthy boundaries in my workplace, even when not demonstrated by others around me	☐	☐
I believe my value in the workplace is equal to all others regardless of hierarchy	☐	☐

ENVIRONMENTAL	YES	NO
I know how to ground myself and feel connected to the universe	☐	☐
I participate in community activities and I value my contribution	☐	☐
I spend more time outdoors than indoors	☐	☐
I make a conscious effort to spend time in nature more days than not	☐	☐
I believe I am connected to all living systems	☐	☐

SOCIAL	YES	NO
I find the time to connect with people who are important to me every week	☐	☐
I enjoy being amongst people who are different to me	☐	☐
I speak my truth without hesitation amongst all those I know and love	☐	☐
I prioritise my own needs above the needs of others and I find it easy to say no	☐	☐
I own my actions when problems arise between myself and others, and I actively work to better myself	☐	☐

SPIRITUAL	YES	NO
I find it easy to forgive myself and others when I feel pain	☐	☐
If I ask myself the question, 'Who am I?', I know the answer	☐	☐
I have a strong belief in my purpose here in this life	☐	☐
I have faith in a greater power	☐	☐
I know my core values and I find it easy to make decisions that are in line with these values, even when challenged by others	☐	☐

ASPECTS OF WELLNESS	MAXIMUM SCORE	MY SCORE
Physical	5	0
Emotional	5	0
Occupational	5	0
Environmental	5	0
Social	5	0
Spiritual	5	0
TOTAL:		0

SCORES

Less than 18: You feel lost and question who you are. Do you want more for yourself?

18-24: You are on the right path. Are you being called to greater things?

25 and above: Congratulations. You are living an extraordinary life.

If your soul is calling you to greater things, contact us and move forward on your journey.

Your name:_____   Your email: _____

Elm Lodge Wellness Retreats

Are you trapped in the expectations of others?

Are you feeling lost and wondering who you really are?

Are you ready to awaken your spirit and live your most extraordinary life?

Finding power in your pain is the key to transformation. Your greatest weaknesses are the pathway to your greatest strengths. When you learn to embrace the challenges of your life you will embrace the truth of your wounds and release yourself from the suffering that causes both mental and physical illness.

At our signature **Elm Lodge Wellness Retreats**, we combine the powerful combination of shamanic healing and holistic psychology where we work with you to release the suffering of your human existence and reconnect with your heart space, where we find unconditional love, joy, and self-fulfilment. You are your greatest healer.

This unique experience, by application only, is the next level in healing and connection. For more details on these retreats, and to claim your $100 off Gift-Certificate, visit www.elmlodgewellness.com.au

CODE: **DROPTHEACT** for $100 discount

glanceypsych@gmail.com

www.kateglancey.com   www.elmlodgewellness.com.au

KATE GLANCEY

Kate Glancey is a highly sought-after Psychologist in the Macarthur Region of South-West Sydney. She has more than 24 years' experience in private practice and is a published author of the book, Drop The Act. She has had a remarkable impact on hundreds of people and has played an integral role in their journey towards improved quality of life.

After facing her own greatest challenge she embarked on a journey of personal growth. Whilst on this journey she discovered that from her greatest weaknesses came her greatest strengths. Through the gifts of her own struggles, she came to accept that ordinary was no longer enough.

Over the last five years Kate has facilitated holistic wellness programs with her partner, where the power of holistic psychology together with shamanic energy healing has assisted many individuals transform their own lives.

An engaging and relatable speaker, the wisdom shared through Kate's real-life accounts are inspirational and uplifting. Her story telling is both personable and down to earth and will empower you to become the creator of your own existence and live the freedom of an extraordinary life.

Kate's signature talks include:

6 Steps to Living and Extraordinary Life
- Find your bliss
- Turn pain into purpose
- Unleash your superpowers

How to Get Everything You Want in Life
- Become a conscious creator
- Burn your bridges
- Live in gratitude and joy

Transform Ordinary into Extraordinary
- Release the suffering
- Heal the wounds
- Live your purpose

✉ glanceypsych@gmail.com

🌐 www.kateglancey.com 🌐 www.elmlodgewellness.com.au

REFERENCES

———————— ♦ ◇ ♦ ————————

Brené Brown, May 24, 2018, *The Midlife Unraveling*, accessed *8.9.2022* brenebrown.com/articles/2018/05/24/the-midlife-unraveling/[1]

Roxanne Hai 2012 *Being Vulnerable about vulnerability: Q&A with Brené Brown*, accessed 8.9.2022 blog.ted.com/being-vulnerable-about-vulnerability-qa-with-brene-brown/amp/[2]

Oxford Languages, Google[3]

Winston Churchill, 1906 *Under-Secretary of the Colonial Office* accessed 8.9.2022

En.m.wikipedia.org/wiki/With_great_power_comes_great_responsibility[4]

REFLECTIONS

Drop The Act

Reflections

www.ingramcontent.com/pod-product-compliance
Lightning Source LLC
Chambersburg PA
CBHW030300100526
44590CB00012B/458